Allan Massie

Allan Massie was born in Singapore in 1938. He is
the author of twelve novels, including THE LAST
PEACOCK, winner of the Frederick Niven Award in
1981, A QUESTION OF LOYALTIES, winner of the
Saltire/*Scotsman* Book of the Year, THE SINS OF THE
FATHER, THESE ENCHANTED WOODS and THE
RAGGED LION. AUGUSTUS is the first of a trilogy of
Roman novels followed by TIBERIUS, then CAESAR.
His non-fiction books include BYRON'S TRAVELS, a
biography of Colette and a book on Edinburgh. He is also
a columnist for the *Daily Telegraph* and is the lead fiction
reviewer for *The Scotsman*. Allan Massie is a Fellow of
the Royal Society of Literature and lives in the Scottish
borders, near Scott's home at Abbotsford.

D1150788

S

SCEPTRE

Also by Allan Massie

Novels

Change and Decay in All Around I See
The Last Peacock
The Death of Men
One Night in Winter
Augustus
A Question of Loyalties
Tiberius
The Sins of the Father
Caesar
The Ragged Lion
These Enchanted Woods

Non-Fiction

Muriel Spark
Ill-Met by Gaslight
The Caesars
Portrait of Scottish Rugby
Colette
101 Great Scots
Byron's Travels
Glasgow: Portrait of a City
The Novel Today 1970–89
Edinburgh

King David

ALLAN MASSIE

SCEPTRE

British Library Cataloguing in Publication Data

Massie, Allan
  King David
  I. Title
  823.914 [F]

ISBN 0 340 65990 4

Typeset by Palimpsest Book Production Limited,
Polmont, Stirlingshire
Printed and bound in Great Britain by
Cox and Wyman Ltd, Reading, Berkshire

Hodder and Stoughton
A division of Hodder Headline PLC
338 Euston Road
London NW1 3BH

First, for Alison:
then, for Robert Nye

List of Characters

HOUSE OF DAVID

DAVID	Second King of Israel, son of Jesse, mayor of Bethlehem
JESSE	His father
SHAMMAH	His favourite brother, and officer
ELIAB ABINADAB	His other brothers, and officers
ZERUIAH	His half-sister, mother of Joab, Asahel and Abishai
MICHAL	Daughter of Saul, wife of David
BATHSHEBA	Granddaughter of Achitophel, wife of Uriah and, later, of David; mother of Solomon
ABIGAIL	Widow of landowner, Nabal, and wife of David
AHINOAM	Her waiting-woman, and mistress of David; mother of Amnon
MAACAH	Arab daughter of Talmai, King of Geshur, wife of David; mother of Absalom and Tamar
HAGGITH	Mother of David's son Adonijah
AMNON	David's first son, by Ahinoam
ABSALOM	David's favourite son, by Maacah
SOLOMON	David's least favourite son, by Bathsheba, who succeeds him as king
TAMAR	David's most beautiful daughter, by Maacah
ADONIJAH	David's son, by Haggith
JOAB	David's nephew, who deserts Saul to become commander of his army
ABISHAI ASAHEL	Nephews and officers of David
JONADAB	Nephew, chamberlain and confidant of David

AMASA	David's nephew and aide-de-camp who becomes commander of Absalom's rebel army
LAISH	Shepherd-boy; David's catamite who becomes his armour-bearer
ABISHAG	A Shunnamite; concubine of David in old age
AZREEL	David's servant, put to death by him for the murder of Nehemiah, a sergeant of Jonathan's army
HUSHAI	An Archite who becomes David's most trusted clerk
BENAIAH	Commander of David's guard
AHIMAAZ	Son of the High Priest Abiathar
NATHAN	A prophet at David's court

HOUSE OF SAUL

SAUL	First King of Israel, of the tribe of Benjamin
JONATHAN	His son, a heroic soldier and David's close friend
ISHBOSHETH	His other son, whom Abner appoints as Saul's successor
MICHAL	His daughter, wife of David
MERAB	His other daughter
ABNER	His cousin, commander of his bodyguard and his most famous general
SHIMEI	His cousin and David's enemy
MEPHIBOSHETH	Crippled son of Jonathan, adopted by David
ADONIJAH	Officer of Saul and friend of Jonathan
ACHITOPHEL	Sage; member first of Saul's, and then of David's, council before becoming adviser to Absalom in his rebellion
NEHEMIAH	Sergeant of Jonathan
ELHANAN	One of Joab's soldiers whose murder provokes the killing of Asahal
DOEG	An Edomite, once the servant of Saul, to whom he betrays David

LEVITES

ELI	High Priest of Shiloh, teacher of Samuel
SAMUEL	Hebrew prophet, seer and judge, who succeeds Eli
ABIMELECH	Eli's grandson, a priest

ABIATHAR	His son; high priest
ZADOK	High Priest
JEHOSHAPHAT ⎫	Priests, scribes
SENAIAH ⎭	

OTHERS

GOLIATH	Giant champion of the Philistines
URIAH	First husband of Bathsheba; a Hittite officer in David's bodyguard and a spy for Achitophel
RECHAB ⎫	Murderers of Ishbosheth
NAANAN ⎭	
NABAL	Landowner from Carmel
ACHISH	Philistine King of Gath
AGAG	King of the Amalekites
HIRAM	Phoenician King of Tyre
NAHASH	King of Ammon
HANUN	His son

Book 1 ∫

Because I am cold and shiver at night, they have procured for me this young girl, Abishag, a Shunnamite, that she may share my bed and bring me warmth. She is a nice girl and pretty, plump and smooth-skinned as young olives. Well trained too in the use of her cherry lips and warm hands. She evinces no repugnance as she presses her youth against my cold leathery body which is almost that of a corpse. She works in silence and tenderly, with the art that is either natural or the result of good schooling; but I cannot respond.

Old age is a shipwreck. Sometimes in the middle of the night, denied sleep, I listen to her breathing and find myself in tears.

She hesitates to speak. I do not know if she is full of questions which she does not dare to put to me. I am impressed by her soft restraint, and if I was a sentimental man, I would read love in her tenderness. But of course there is no love, and could not be. When I was young, the thought of such a girl consorting with the withered and flaccid thing I have become, would have filled me with disgust. Even now, I feel pity for her, sufficient at least to guard her from the fear that corrupts my spirit.

I lay my hand between her thighs and dream wakefully of the past.

It is impossible that my son Solomon, who enters my room every morning in the hope that he will find himself king, should understand me, for he has been nurtured delicately in palaces, his skin never exposed to harsh weather, whilst I was reared in adversity among the mountains. I resent this difference, and dislike him for it. Of all my sons I feel least for him, and yet he will be my heir because I am old and cannot oppose his mother Bathsheba, whom I once loved more than any of my wives, except Michal, Saul's daughter, who turned against me, as I have turned against Bathsheba now, though too weary and feeble to oppose her will.

Solomon does not know what it is to be cold, exposed to wind and rain and snow, listening to the wolves howling in the fringes of the night. He has never known solitude, nor felt himself to be no more than a speck in the immensity of the wilderness. He has never listened to the Lord's words in the wind. How can he be king, as I have been?

I was the youngest and most beautiful of my father's sons, the child of his old age and his favourite. My brothers hated me, all but Shammah, as Joseph's brothers had hated him in his coat of many colours. For my part I envied them because they had escaped the herding and gone to the army to join themselves to the great King Saul. I made up stories in the night, and now I do not know which were true and which imaginary. Did I really kill a lion and a wolf as I boasted of doing? Perhaps. But I am a poet and poets are liars who praise the Almighty for the fertility of His creation.

But I did not imagine Samuel.

I knew of him only as the High Priest, the servant of the Lord and a man whose wrath was famous throughout Judah.

When he sent word to my father Jesse, as mayor of Bethlehem, that he purposed to lodge with us when he came to sacrifice to the Lord in our little town, I was glad to have the excuse to slip away to the hills to tend the sheep. I cared nothing for priests, and, since it was the lambing season, much for the well-being of my flock.

My brothers however were eager to see the High Priest, and quarrelled among themselves as to which should receive his blessing.

"And why should he wish to bless any of you?" I inquired, and had my ears boxed.

"These are matters beyond the understanding of a little shepherd," they said.

It was a spring morning of the utmost beauty. Towards noon I gathered the ewes in the shade of an olive grove, and lay there tranquil, with my arm round the rough neck of one of the dogs. The sun was warm on my legs and the young lambs played, and every now and then a ewe bleated to recall one that had strayed too far. I drank wine mixed with water from my goatskin flask, and ate bread and cheese which I shared with the dogs.

The sunlight flickered through the olive branches, and the world was good and at peace. I turned over the lines of a poem I was making in praise of the beauty of the earth and the bounty of the Lord's creation. All my life I have been happiest in solitude, under the heavens, for it is only then that everything is still and time's motion seems arrested.

I murmured my name, "David, David, David," lovingly, and it seemed to me that it spread over the hillside and filled the world. "The earth is the Lord's and the fullness thereof," and I was granted its complete enjoyment.

Even then I knew that it was not my allotted task to measure out my days in the care of flocks and herds, or in counting sheaves at harvest, but that a nobler destiny awaited me. And because I knew this, I felt no impatience, but delighted in the performance of my humble task, and in the opportunities for thought and reverie which solitude offered me. I have always distrusted and despised the man who cannot bear to be alone.

We are creatures of such odd contrivance that this content sat easily alongside my envy for my brothers in the army.

I felt even then my powers and the wind in the olive leaves brought me the promise of glory.

The sound of footsteps scrambling up the hillside broke in on my dreaming. The dog's birse stiffened under my hand, and he growled a low warning. I pressed on him to restrain a bark, and got to my feet, ready for any encounter.

It was my brother Shammah, hot and panting, and for the moment unable to speak. I passed him my goatskin and he refreshed himself, and smiled.

"Well," he said, "there are strange goings-on down there, and no mistake."

He drank again and returned the flask to me.

"I've been sent to fetch you," he said.

"That's silly," I said. "I can't leave the sheep. Father knows that."

"That's all right," he said, "if you look down the hill, you'll see old Gideon struggling up to take your place."

"But what's happening?"

"Well, that's a mystery," he said. "Samuel arrived."

"What's he like?"

"What you might expect. Alarming. The village council were nervous. 'Have you come in peace?' they said. They looked as if they would have barred his entry if they had dared."

"But why? He's the High Priest. They should have been honoured."

"You're an innocent, young David, lost in your dreams and poetry and sheep, you don't really know anything, do you? I wish Gideon would hurry up."

"He's an old man. It's an effort, that hill. Anyway, I can't see . . . but go on, tell me more."

"They were nervous and scared, but they couldn't refuse to admit him, seeing he is, as you say, the High Priest, so he performed his sacrifice – and I don't know why he had to come to Bethlehem to do that, but then I don't understand the priests – and then the elders were dismissed, without much ceremony I must say, and he came into our house. Even you may have noticed, little brother, what a state the women were in, and they were worse when Samuel refused to eat and said he had business to conclude first. What business, you may well ask, as we all did. Then he made Father parade us one by one before him, and I don't mind telling you, David, it was unnerving, the way he looked at me, as if he saw right into my heart, mind, and soul. And then he felt me all over like I was a colt he was thinking of buying, and grunted heavily, and looked me in the eye again, and shook his head and pushed me away. But then he called me back, as if he was thinking of making an offer – the way you might do at a market – and he put his hand under my chin and forced me to meet his gaze. I tell you, I didn't like it, I felt the sweat running down the back of my legs. But he sighed and grunted again, and said to Father, 'Are these all your sons? Don't you have another?' So Father said there was only the youngest, who was tending the sheep. 'Tending the sheep,' said Samuel, in a wondering sort of way, or maybe more suspicious, 'tending the sheep? Fetch him to me.' There's something terrible about him, you know, an air of authority or power, though he's only an old man, you might think. 'Fetch him at once, for we shall neither eat nor drink till I have seen him." The women murmured and moaned, thinking of the dinner being spoiled, and he may have heard them, for he glowered and said, 'For such is the will of the Lord.' So here I am, and here at last is Gideon to relieve you, and we'd better hurry for I can't answer for his temper or our mother's if we delay."

And so I descended the hillside, and entered the house. For a moment, coming in out of the sun, I could see nothing and felt dizzy because I had been running, and the world swam about me. But a hand seized me and held me, and the darkness cleared, and I saw Samuel and fell to my knees before him.

He placed his hand under my chin, rough against smooth, and forced it upwards so that my eyes were compelled to meet his. The smell of old flesh was rank and sour as a billy-goat's. He held me, and commanded the company to depart.

We were alone, and his silence, his smell, and some strange emanation of power oppressed me. A donkey brayed in the courtyard, and still Samuel did not speak.

He withdrew a horn of oil from within the folds of his cloak, and poured some on my head, and worked the oil, which was sickly scented, with his thumb into my skull. He muttered words which I could not understand. They were, I know now, in the Old Tongue which only the priests speak, though many of them today do not themselves comprehend the meaning of their antique incantations.

He drew me up, and kissed me on both cheeks, and on the mouth, holding me in a fierce embrace as his nails dug into the skin over my ribs.

"Child," he said, "I have consecrated you the servant of the Lord of Hosts, and the instrument of his vengeance."

Then he called my father and said to him:

"Blessed are you among fathers for the boy David is the chosen of the Lord."

And when we came to eat, he placed me at his right hand, in the seat of honour, and plied me with wines and the daintiest of meats.

"I see," he said, "that this boy David is as virtuous as he is beautiful, and so he has found favour with the Lord and with me his humble minister."

I thought, with sudden horror: he hasn't selected me to be a priest, has he? But that thought passed, for even then I knew that only those from the tribe of Levi can be priests.

He drank wine and pressed the same cup to my lips, and his gaze rested on my legs naked under my short tunic. He stroked my cheeks and I felt myself flush as I saw my brothers Eliab and Abinadab nudge each other and snigger to see the old man languish over me.

Then, with some excuse, seeing Samuel affected by wine, my father drew me aside and told me to return to my flock.

"There are things that have happened here today that must be kept secret," he said.

Shammah slipped from the house with me, and we began to climb the hill as the light failed. I told him all that had passed, and he was silent for a long time. Then he stretched out his hand and touched my head, and ran his fingers through my hair, and carried them to his lips and smelled them.

"The holy oil of the Lord. David, I am afraid for you."

"Shammah," I said, "I do not understand you. I understand nothing of what has happened today. Perhaps I dare not understand."

"There is no question," he said. "It can mean only one thing."

I recalled the sniggers of Eliab and Abinadab.

I tried to joke.

"Our brothers seemed to think they knew what was happening."

"They are fools. David," he said, "I fear for you. You are the Anointed of Israel, anointed with oil as Saul the King was anointed."

The sun slipped behind the mountains.

"Saul is the King," I said, "and he has sons."

"That is what makes me afraid," he said.

We dismissed Gideon, and counted the sheep, and then Shammah slept. But I lay wakeful under the stars and, though I shivered, there was strange music in my heart. I drew my hands through my hair, and they smelled still of the holy oil of Israel.

2

Our history is written by the priests, for which reason I have troubled myself never to offend them. Samuel was the High Priest and is therefore its hero, or will be. But it was more complicated than that. The choice of hero depends on the person choosing. That visit of Samuel's determined my life. I owe what I am to his favour, though it came close to bringing me death. It is pointless to speculate what would have become of me if the Lord had not directed his gaze to fall on me, but now, when so little matters, let me tell it as it was.

Samuel then, first: the child of the Temple in Shiloh, given by his mother to the service of the Lord and Eli the High Priest. He was soon Eli's favourite among the temple-boys, and comforted him, they say, as Abishag comforts me. But that may be only malicious rumour, such as priests attract on account of their love of secrecy, and I do not know whether the boy Samuel was Eli's catamite or not. Our priests are not forbidden women, as the priests of some nations are, but Eli, it is said, consorted with no woman after the birth of his sons Hophni and Phineas.

Certainly, too, he had need of comfort, for Hophni and Phineas sinned against the Lord, and lay with whores who frequented the precincts of the Temple, and committed various abominations, widely condemned.

Be that as it may, what was of greater urgency was their failure to perform the first duty of those who govern a state: to secure it and its people against their enemies. So, in Eli's time, the Philistines ranged freely throughout Israel, and carried off the

Ark of the Covenant, to the shame of Eli and all the Children of Israel.

It will be hard for any now to comprehend how the name of the Philistines spread terror in Israel, so completely have I subdued and subjugated them. For my part, though I have slain so many, I never shared the common prejudice against this people. On the contrary, I saw that we had much to learn from them. They were skilled in arts of which we were ignorant, and incomparably more civilised than the rough tribes of Israel of my youth. Yet, since they lacked a god or gods capable of protecting them, they reaped a bitter harvest at my hands.

Samuel pleased Eli, no matter how, and succeeded him as Judge over Israel. I shall not recount in detail his years of power; they may be read, favourably presented, in the writings of the priests, and should therefore be read with caution.

Samuel's sons were as incompetent and disreputable as Eli's had been. Priests ascribe great wisdom to themselves, but it is remarkable how seldom their children walk in the way of the Lord.

So a deputation of the chief men of every tribe came to Samuel. They complained of his sons' failure to guard Israel, and demanded an end to priestly rule. "Israel should have a king, like other nations," they said.

This sensible request drove Samuel to fury. He told them that a king would be a tyrant, and he threatened all sorts of terrible fates if the people were so misguided as to prefer a king to the holy government of priests. There would be conscription, and taxation, and seduction of daughters.

His eloquence did not convince them. The experience of, first Eli's sons, and then Samuel's, made them think no king could be worse.

So Samuel gave way, knowing that if he did not they would ignore him and choose a king for themselves. It was better, he reasoned, to choose one whom he could control.

He delayed as long as he could. This candidate was not right, that was rejected by the Lord, and so on. At last he selected Saul, the son of Kish, of the tribe of Benjamin.

I have heard much argument as to why he settled on Saul,

but, having made his decision, he insisted that the Lord had guided him. Later he was to regret saying so, but at the time it seemed wise to him. The Lord spoke through Samuel; Samuel had nominated Saul. Therefore, it was clear, the King was subservient to the High Priest.

That is the sort of argument that appeals to priests, but of course, whatever its attractions, it can lead to a a conclusion which is ridiculous and unworkable.

Saul was very handsome in his youth, tall and nobly built, with long curling black hair and sad brown eyes. He spoke in a low voice and his lips were cherry-red. Samuel anointed him with oil, kissed him, and told him that the Lord had made him captain of His people Israel.

"You are the Sword of the Lord, the Sword of Israel, as I am its Judge, and the interpreter of His will."

Poor Saul was horrified. He had come to Samuel only to seek his help in retrieving some asses of his father's which had strayed or been stolen. The last thing he wanted was to be made king.

"The tribe of Benjamin," he protested, "is the smallest of all the tribes, we are humble hill-folk, and my father is not even one of the chief men of Benjamin."

Samuel smiled. What of that, his smile said, when I, Samuel, the instrument of the Lord, have named you King?

"It is the will of the Lord," he said, and so Saul had no choice but to do as he was bid. He did not realise that the insignificance of his family and tribe was one reason for his selection.

Years later, his son, my dearest friend Jonathan, from whom I learned of Saul's dismay, told me that Saul's mother had wept when word was brought that he had been named King.

"No good will come of it," she said; a prophecy that preyed on Jonathan's mind and made him believe that he was himself destined to die young.

Soon however the idea of being king excited Saul. In any case, after his anointing, there was no knowing what Samuel would do in his anger if Saul rejected the honour.

Yet, Jonathan said, Saul was unhappy for a long time after his elevation. He didn't know what was expected of him – nor, I suppose, did anyone else – and he was greatly in awe of Samuel, who rarely left him alone, one moment stroking his cheek and telling him he was the favourite of the Lord, and the next, fixing him with his mad protuberant blue eyes and treating him like an ignorant and erring child.

Saul's later troubles were the consequence of this early uncertainty. He lacked self-confidence and would veer from one extreme to another. Despite his great talents, he never fully believed in his right to be king. He knew that Samuel resented the necessity of his appointment, even while he treated him as his minion or toy.

There was one thing, however, that Samuel hadn't reckoned on. Saul proved himself a natural leader of men, and a general with a rare eye for country and a good understanding of the principles of war. I should like to state here that, though my own military renown was greatly to surpass Saul's, I learned much of my craft from him. In his early days, before his mind grew clouded and his judgement impaired, he was a master of the art of war. This confounded Samuel, and irritated him, however pleasing the results might be for Israel, because he could see Saul escaping his tutelage. The truth is, the old priest was consumed by jealousy.

This was soon made manifest in disgraceful fashion. Engaged against the Philistines, Saul lured their army to a pass where they were compelled to give battle in unfavourable circumstances. Saul then sent for Samuel that he might offer sacrifices to the Lord. Samuel did not respond. Saul delayed. The army became restive. Some said that the Lord did not favour the enterprise; others showed their doubts by slipping away and setting off for home. Again Saul sent for Samuel; again the old man made no reply. Whereupon, losing patience, and fearing the effect which further delay would have, Saul boldly conducted the service and offered the sacrifices himself.

No sooner had he done so than a flourish of trumpets indicated the arrival of Samuel. He gazed on the slaughtered beasts, whose blood was still flowing; and he gazed on Saul. The King did not flinch. This angered the priest still more greatly, for he saw that Saul had escaped his authority. He raised his hands on high, and cursed Saul for his impatience and impiety. The Lord, he said, who had intended to establish Saul's kingdom over Israel for ever and ever, now deplored the King's irreverence. He had withdrawn His favour from Saul, as a cloud may obscure the sun.

Saul tried to explain. It was no good. The Lord, Samuel told him, prized obedience more than the fat of rams.

Nevertheless, when battle was joined, Saul was victorious. People began to wonder if Samuel could indeed interpret the Lord's will correctly.

No doubt these whisperings came to the old man's ears. They intensified his hatred of Saul. I understand his feelings; few things are more bitter than a love that has died. Samuel had loved Saul when he thought him his creature. Now that Saul had escaped him, Samuel reproached himself for his former love.

All this of course I know only by report, but I have no doubt, from my knowledge of both Saul and Samuel, how things stood between them. Saul was dismayed. He had revered Samuel and luxuriated in his favour. Its withdrawal distressed him. He believed he had acted wisely; yet the fear of the Lord was strong in him, and he never doubted (as others did) that Samuel was the mouthpiece of the Lord. And yet Saul did not see how he could have acted otherwise.

Their last meeting was still more bitter. The Amalekites, in alliance with the Kenites, were pressing hard on the southern frontiers of Israel. Despite his previous experience, Saul again sought Samuel's blessing. It was given, but with this rider: "Go and smite Amalek," Samuel said, "and utterly destroy all that they have, every man, woman and child, and all their flocks and herds."

It is not clear how Saul understood this message. In my opinion, he thought it typical priestly rhetoric. At any rate, when he had achieved victory, after taking the sensible precaution of bribing the King of the Kenites to desert his ally, he was satisfied with a crushing success, and made no attempt to follow Samuel's instructions. He understood, as I have always done, that extreme measures are suitable only in extremity. He wished, I suppose, to pacify the southern frontier, not to arouse undying hostility to Israel.

Samuel arrived in the camp at Gilgal. He asked Saul to account for the lowing of oxen and bleating of sheep around the camp.

"Are those not the flocks and herds of the Amalekites, which the Lord ordered should be destroyed?"

Saul admitted that they were, and, still trying to appease Samuel, said that the old man could select the best to be sacrificed to the Lord. (This was generous of him, since the flesh of sacrificial animals is a perquisite of the priests.) Samuel was not appeased. Saul had defied him once too often; he had set his own judgement above the Lord's. Therefore the Lord had rejected Saul as King of Israel.

Saul must have sighed to hear this, but gave (I am told) the impression of being unmoved. After all, whatever Samuel's prestige, Saul's own was now greater, on account of his victories. He knew perfectly well that the army would follow and obey him, not Samuel. Soldiers rarely have a high opinion of priests, and, though Saul's army was mostly composed of conscripts and part-time volunteers, he had by this time formed the nucleus of a professional force in the Royal Guard, devoted to his own person. Whatever the moral effect of Samuel's curses, the immediate practical consequences must have seemed negligible.

All the same he still thought it better to try to restore good relations with Samuel. So when the old man commanded that the King of the Amalekites should be brought before him, Saul sent to his own tent where he had lodged him. I don't know what he expected to happen. I don't know what I would have expected in his position. Probably he thought that the old man would rave and curse in the fashion with which Saul had become tiresomely acquainted. At any rate he can't have expected that Samuel would snatch up a sword and hack at the unfortunate King Agag's neck. Saul leapt up to intervene and knocked the sword out of the old man's grasp. He told him to get out of the camp and to consider himself lucky to be allowed to do so. When a few days later Agag died of his wounds, the Queen of the Amalekites demanded that Samuel be tried for murder. Saul refused. It would all have been too embarrassing. Instead he gave the Queen one of his own sons – I cannot now remember which – as a husband.

He had handled a difficult situation with a dexterity I can only admire. Samuel was however still more furious to learn that he owed his life to Saul's good sense and clemency.

He retired to Ramah, his own city, where he felt himself secure. Yet, because he had formed the intention of destroying Saul, he could not believe, despite the evidence to the contrary, that Saul harboured no such evil intent towards him. So for some months he did not dare to leave Ramah. As he brooded over what had happened, his bitterness grew sharper, for he saw there was no chance of supplanting Saul in the near future, the King's fame and popularity being so great.

I have no doubt that Samuel really believed that the Lord spoke through him, and that he knew precisely what was in the Lord's mind; so for a long time he remained in perplexity on account of his impotence. It was intolerable to know that the Lord had rejected Saul, and yet to see Saul still flourish.

Still, revenge is a dish to be eaten cold. Samuel told himself that he could die happy, if he knew he had prepared the way for Saul's destruction.

So he consulted priests secretly throughout the land, and communed with the Lord in the watches of the night. Then, having weighed the matter thoroughly, he made the journey to my father's house in Bethlehem, with the results I have already described.

3

Two years passed. There was no word from Samuel, yet I knew that Shammah had been right in his judgement of the significance of what had happened. I had many moments of impatience during this time; yet on the whole I was content to wait. I was at an age when the present moment seems eternal. I delighted in my daily life. There were wars and rumours of wars, but they did not disturb us. When the grass grew I led the flocks to their summer pastures in the hills. Every day my body and mind grew more powerful, and in the evenings I sang, to the accompaniment of my harp, of the glory of God and the wonders of the world around me. My brothers came and went to the wars, and brought back stories of the greatness of Saul and the exploits of his son Jonathan, and of Abner, Saul's cousin and great commander, all drawn from his own tribe of Benjamin. My brothers seemed to have forgotten Samuel's visit, though Eliab called me in angry moments "the priest's boy". Since I knew this to be ridiculous, I remained silent. Only Shammah looked at me in a different way.

And then came other stories: that Saul had been stricken with a strange illness that disturbed his mind and cast him into melancholy that was near despair. When people talked about the King's state, they remembered how Samuel had cursed him, and they said that the Lord had withdrawn his favour from Saul, and that this was the cause of his madness. At such moments Shammah would lay his hand upon me to urge me to remain silent. But I felt no temptation to speak. If we were right, and the Lord had indeed chosen me, through the mediation of Samuel, then the Lord would in time arrange the means whereby His choice would be made manifest to Israel.

I prized my chastity in those days. It seemed to me that some virtue would depart from me if I yielded to the temptations that I now see are normal. Often in the dark nights I wrestled with my desire, picturing its satisfaction; but not even Rachel, the daughter of our headman, a girl a year my senior who followed my movements about the yard with dark admiring doe-eyes, could tempt me to break the vow which I had made under the stars. Instead I poured out my heart in poetry, and the beauty and melody of my songs won me celebrity and new admirers.

At last there came a day when I was again summoned from the hills. I found my father with a dark young man perhaps seven years older than myself. He was tall and thin with a black scented beard and a long nose that wrinkled at the tip.

"He stinks of sheep and goats," he said.

The man's left eye was not set straight, and he looked across that long nose at me.

"Still, that can be remedied," he said, "when we arrive at Gibeah."

"David," my father said, "this is your sister's son Joab who has come to take you to the King. Saul is sick, troubled in his mind, and his physicians have recommended that music may soothe his spirit. Go, therefore, and fetch your harp, for you are to set out as soon as possible, and ride through the night."

I knew of Joab from my brothers' conversation. His mother was the child of my father's first wife, and he was their equal in age, younger indeed than the eldest of them, but had already far surpassed them in renown. They spoke of him jealously, but with reluctant admiration.

"It is a great honour that you have been chosen," my father said; but I could tell that he was both puzzled and anxious.

"I myself am responsible," Joab said. "My mother has often spoken of the boy's musical gifts." He sniffed. "It is not something I either know about or care for. Nevertheless when they were seeking a musician, I remembered what she had said, and put his name forward. I shall be grateful if the boy does me no discredit."

My father had already ordered the servants to prepare gifts to take to the King. These were homely things: some of the finest bread, a couple of kids and an amphora of wine from last year's vintage. Joab showed signs of impatience and I hurried off to fetch my harp, first wrapping it in the leaves of wild lilies to protect it from the cold of the night and the heat of the morning sun. My feelings were mixed. I was delighted to find the world opening before me. On the other hand I had never expected that I would enter it in the guise of a harpist.

We set off in silence, and silence was maintained for the first stage of the journey. I was conscious that the ass I was riding cut a mean figure beside Joab's mule, and that the long nose silhouetted against the night sky seemed to insist on my inferiority to its owner. Yet I refused to be subdued. There was exhilaration in the movement of the hoofs and the clink of the armour of Joab's guard. The moon rose over the mountains, the air grew cold, and night fell as we picked our way along the rough path that skirted the hills.

Towards dawn we saw Jerusalem across the valley. The city, it is perhaps necessary to say, was still in those days the stronghold of the Jebusites, a tribe that had never acknowledged the supremacy of Israel.

"Why," I asked Joab, "do we suffer the enemies of the Lord to occupy such a fine place?"

"The city is well fortified," Joab said. "How, little boy, would you suggest that we take it?"

I resented his tone, but I was determined not to show my feelings. So I merely smiled and said in as friendly a tone as I could muster that of course I would hesitate to put forward any suggestion, having no experience in such matters, and knowing full well that nothing I said could be of any interest to one who had achieved as much as my cousin had. (He was of course actually my nephew, but I thought it more politic to call him cousin.) I would however be most interested to hear how he would approach the problem, for I was eager to learn, and unwilling to lose the opportunity of doing so which this journey so unexpectedly offered. As I spoke I could sense Joab unbend; I have always found that flattery breaches the defences established by pride. I knew this by instinct, and my instinct was now confirmed by experience, for Joab at once launched himself into a detailed analysis of the military problems which my question raised, and by the time he had finished speaking, I knew that I had elevated myself in his estimation. People are generally far happier to give their opinion than to listen to the views of others, and Joab was no exception. Nothing gives great men a higher notion of the intelligence of others than to be fed with admiring questions. When Joab had finished his exposition, which was, I may say, lucid and interesting, he had so far altered his opinion of me that he told me I might make a soldier yet. And actually I had said nothing to make him think so; I had only allowed him full rein.

4

Joab left me in an anteroom in the palace. I was happy to be relieved of his presence, and I think he felt the same. His manner had softened in the course of our journey, but now that we had arrived, he was, I fancy, embarrassed. He was a stiff, conventional man, and though he may, as he said, have suggested that I might be the person to help or heal the King, nevertheless he may also have felt that a singer and harpist did the family little credit. I do not know. I have known Joab all my life but I have never been certain that I could read his mind. There has always been something in him that escapes me. He feels the same about me, and though few have served me better, none has done so less willingly. Life has yoked us together like a pair of oxen in the fields, but that is the most that can be said.

Now I waited and waited. I was nervous, for everything was strange to me. At the same time everything was of the greatest interest. I was being given my first glimpse of the world which I knew myself fitted for, and it impressed me that in all the coming and going no one took any notice of the boy sitting in the corner with his harp at his feet.

A serving-girl brought me cakes and wine, and looked at me as if she would have liked us to speak together. But I was incapable of engaging in the ordinary banter of conversation. Nor could I eat or drink. I felt hollow; there was a great emptiness waiting to be filled, but nothing material would fill it.

At last a stout young man stood before me, and said that Abner wished to see me. I knew who Abner was, of course: his fame ran throughout Israel. The man spoke to me as if I was a servant. I picked up my harp and followed him.

A tall man stood with his back to me. The stout young man spoke and left us. I waited. A trickle of sweat ran down my thigh. It was very warm and the scent of flowers came close to overpowering me. I prayed to the Lord to give me strength.

Abner turned and advanced upon me. He put his hand under my chin, as Samuel had done, and raised it up so that I was compelled to meet his eyes. It was all I could do not to turn away, but he held me steady and gazed on my face as if he sought to draw from me the essence of my soul. It was not what I had expected.

"The Lord knows," he said, "the Lord knows if you will do. Do you understand?" he said. "Has Joab told you what is required of you?"

I gestured towards my harp, but could find no words.

"No," Abner said. "I suppose not. He will have preferred to leave it to me. That is his way. Very well, then," he released my chin, "very well then, young David, the King has taken leave of his wits. In a word, which you will swear to pass on to nobody, if you wish to live to see the sun rise tomorrow, he is mad. He is sunk into gloomy silence, and shakes with terrors which he dare not, or cannot, name. Do you understand anything of this?"

"I have known fear," I said. "At night, in the mountains, alone, I have felt the nakedness of my soul."

"Hmmph," he said. "I don't know what that means. Are you afraid now?"

"Yes," I said, "but I trust in the Lord."

"I don't know about that either," he said, "but we'll have to try. He may be violent, I warn you, but his physicians seem to think that music may calm him. That's why you're here."

He poured himself a mug of wine, and drank.

"The King is a great man," he said. "Remember that, though he will appear to you a hollow shell."

*   *   *

The room was like a cavern, and the single oil-lamp shed a meagre light, which left most of the chamber in shadow. There was a powerful odour of burning herbs. (Later I learned that the King's physicians believed this might alleviate his headaches.) For a moment it seemed to be deserted. Then I was aware of a shape crouched on the floor, with its back to the wall, near the table on which the lamp stood. It lifted its head, and as my eyes became accustomed to the gloom, they met the King's, dull as if they saw nothing, yet steady as if they penetrated my very soul. The King's eyes remained fixed on me as I crouched and began to tune my harp. I kept my own gaze averted, but I could not escape the consciousness of that sullen glare.

Abner had warned me that there would be no conversation, and so I touched the strings of the harp and began to sing.

I was accustomed to sing alone, under the night sky, for myself, for an affirmation of the beauty of creation; and I had often sung in our village in the evening while the serving-girls clustered round and crooned the chorus and gazed at me with an admiration that caused me to modulate the mood, shifting from ardour to melancholy regret, which drew forth their tears and deep sighing. Then I knew myself to be master not only of the music but of all who heard it. But now when I began to sing to Saul, my throat was dry, my voice thin, and I played three wrong notes in the first ballad. But he did not stir. I sang of Abraham and the morning of our race, of Joseph and his greatness in Egypt, of Moses and the crossing of the Red Sea and the years in the wilderness, of Joshua and the sound of the trumpets that brought down the walls of Jericho; and Saul did not stir.

My voice strengthened but my heart beat faster, for I saw the prospect of failure yawning before me. I saw this great opportunity which had been vouchsafed me cast ingloriously away. I heard the taunts of my brothers and I pictured myself returning in ignominy to my father's house. I could have cried in pain like a wounded animal, and in my heart I cursed this thing that was, or had been, Saul, that he would not respond to my music, but remained insensible as the rocks among the mountains.

I sang of love, of maidens at the well as the evening lengthened and they looked with longing at the herdsmen who had come there before them. I sang the tender beauty of their advances and withdrawals as the moon rose and the donkeys stood under the olive trees. And Saul did not stir.

I wet my lips, and, daring all, sang of the beauty and strength of Saul himself in his glorious youth. I sang his greatness in war and magnanimity in victory.

> High ambition and deeds and the crowning of all
> The blaze of delight that descends on the greatest of all,
> The splendour of morning, the days that enthrall,
> The glory and beauty that brings forth King Saul.

At these words, the head was lifted again. A hand – strong, dark, hairy – stretched forth, stretched out and touched my cheek. His fingers trembled like a woman's in the first moments of awakening passion, but they were cold as metal on a frosty morning. I all but drew away. Instead I forced myself to meet his gaze, and found nothing there. The hand fell away, and I resumed my song. But there was a difference now; the rage was departing from Saul. I crooned a lullaby as one might to a bairn, and the lids fell over those dead eyes, and Saul slept. It was, I knew, the sleep of an exhausted man who for a long time had not dared to let himself slip into unconsciousness for fear of the demons that would assail him. I continued to sing, gently, soothingly; and then there was silence, but for the King's breathing.

After some little while, the curtain was twitched aside, and Abner beckoned to me.

"The King sleeps," I said.

"It is the first time for days. How will he wake?"

"Who can tell?"

"Have the demons abandoned him?"

"Perhaps they sleep also," I said.

"You have done well. You look drained yourself."

He clapped his hands and a slave-girl brought in wine and a dish of little almond cakes.

To this day I do not know the cause of Saul's disturbance, and I do not know why my music soothed him and seemed to effect a cure. Some of the King's courtiers said his condition was the result of a blow he had received from a Philistine sword months previously; this caused the bone to press on his brain, they said. It may well be true; if so, it is difficult to imagine that music could have had any beneficial effect. Yet it is too much to suppose that the improvement in his condition was only happily coincidental with my playing to him. For my part, I have always thought that Samuel's rejection of Saul played havoc with his mind, arousing strange fears. Perhaps Saul had never truly believed himself worthy of his royal role, and so took refuge from his enhanced sense of inadequacy in these bouts of madness. Such an explanation – though of the kind to be mocked by a plain commonsense sort of man like Joab – makes sense to me, for I know from my own experience how the mind is subject to terrors that reason may dismiss but cannot still.

I played to the King again the next day, and again saw him change from a thing in the grip of terrors he could not name to a man able to close his eyes in peaceful sleep. And so it went on for six days, and people wondered at the change in Saul, but held back, being still afraid. Only Abner was confident that a cure was being effected. Every day he encouraged me, for each time before I entered into Saul's chamber, I was seized with fear myself, since it seemed to me that Saul remained incalculable. Moreover I was afraid that the demons would depart from him and take possession of me. Of course such fears were ridiculous, like the fears of a child, or that dread of the night, when the travel-ler is compelled to look behind him, though he knows and tells himself there can be no one there. Nevertheless a fear which he despises obtains mastery over him. For the first few minutes every day I found it hard to pluck the strings of my harp.

Then on the seventh day, towards evening, I sang a song to the Lord which I had made since my arrival at Gibeah.

The Lord is my shepherd: I shall not want.

He maketh me to lie down in green pastures; he leadeth me beside the still waters.

He restoreth my soul; he leadeth me in the paths of righteousness for his name's sake.

Yea, though I walk in the valley of the shadow of death, I will fear no evil: for thou art with me; thy rod and thy staff, they comfort me.

Thou preparest a table before me in the presence of my foes; my head thou anointest with oil; my cup runneth over.

Surely goodness and mercy shall follow me all the days of my life; and I will dwell in the house of the Lord for ever.

Again, when I had finished singing and the notes of the harp had died away, Saul extended his hand and touched me on the cheek, but this time his fingers were warm and his hand was steady.

"I have been away," he said, "and you have brought me back."

So I left him, my heart full of joy, for I knew that I had succeeded as I had not even dared to dream I might. I told Abner that in my opinion the King was himself again.

When he had thanked me and praised me, he displayed for the first time a lack of assurance. This unsettled me; it wasn't what I had looked for in him. For my part, I found my exhilaration draining away. It is a sensation I have since come to recognise as normal after a great expenditure of spirit. You have to descend from the mountain; it is like the sadness that succeeds the act of love. Everything should be different; yet, as from a leaking tankard, triumph seeps away, and you realise that the world is resuming, is bound to resume, its accustomed tenor. The mood was not new to me even then, but in the anteroom of the palace I knew it more completely than ever before.

Abner left me, with a muttered apology; I think he was glad to be gone, suddenly embarrassed by my presence. I threw myself down on a couch and it was all I could do to restrain my tears. All at once the horizon shortened as if night were closing in on me. A few moments before, I had felt capable of anything; now it was as if I had surrendered all my vitality to Saul. Perhaps my fears were justified, and the evil spirit of despair which had taken possession of him, and from which I had released him, was now invading my soul. I prayed to the Lord that He would not let this come upon me, and then I think I slept.

Perhaps I didn't, perhaps my memory refuses to supply me with the confusion of my mind. By then it was almost dark, and I was still in the grip of melancholy, feeling myself useless, when a slave-girl entered bearing a lamp and followed by two young women.

I scrambled to my feet, and they looked at me, and whispered to each other and giggled.

"I'm sorry," I said, "perhaps I shouldn't be here. I don't know. My lord Abner told me to wait, but that was a long time ago."

"He's very pretty."

This was the shorter of them, a dark stocky girl like so many of our village girls.

"Why do you keep looking at me?" the other said.

"I'm sorry," I said again. Then I swallowed. "It's because I've never seen anyone so beautiful."

The short girl giggled again.

"What impertinence," she said.

But now that I had spoken the words, it was true that I couldn't turn my eyes away from the other. She was tall and slim as a gazelle. Her eyes were dark pools below lids coloured with violet. The pencilled eyebrows arched over them and gave to her appearance an air of ineffable disdain which the red curve of her lips did not deny. She was dressed in white silk with a sash that echoed the colour of those lips, and her fingers were white and thin and innocent of toil. I was conscious that in comparison I looked hot, confused, and coarse. I wanted to hide my hands and I hoped she was not aware of the sweat breaking on my brow, and down the back of my thighs. But at the same time I knew an excitement such as I had never felt before, and I was terrified that she would leave me before I could make some impression on her.

"I am sorry," I said, "if I seem impertinent, but no one can look on you and be unmoved by your beauty."

"Oh, that," she said, "Every young man at court remarks on it, when he dares, and in the same way. I am bored by praise of my looks. We came to thank you."

"And look at you," the other said. She giggled again. "To see what sort of person it is who has achieved what all the physicians failed to do. We're the King's daughters. I'm Merab and this is Michal."

In my youth I was given to daydreams, and now it came to me, as if from the winged seraphs of heaven, that Michal had been sent to me as my reward for curing Saul. I knew the thought to be absurd even as it took possession of me and would not let go. So, with my eyes fast on Michal, I answered her sister.

"I have achieved nothing. At most I am an instrument of the Lord."

"That's silly," Merab said.

"And pretentious," Michal said. "I had so hoped you wouldn't be boring, and now I see that as usual my hope is disappointed."

"I don't think he really means it," Merab said.

"Of course he doesn't. It's just another way of showing off. Very tiresome."

"No," I said, and blushed to find myself contradicting her. "No," I plunged on. "It's not like that. It's just that I don't know what I have done, or rather how I did it. I played the harp and sang, and the King is healed. You can't expect me to believe that it's really anything to do with me. Not me myself. I'm a shepherd-boy," I said, "and I don't understand these things."

"A shepherd-boy, how quaint," Michal said.

"He does rather smell of sheep and goats," her sister said. "It's somewhat disagreeable, Micky."

"Well," I said, "I'm sorry about that, but, you see, I can't understand how the King is cured. It's a miracle, and that's why I say I am only an instrument of the Lord. I'm not making any great claim for myself when I say that. Quite the opposite."

Looking back, how I admire my spontaneous cunning! I was desperate to make an impression on Michal, and I knew, without thinking, that it would be no use pretending to be other than I was. There was too much intelligence in her gaze for me to hope to deceive her. So I played up my difference from everything which she might be acquainted with. I couldn't compete with the scented dandies of the palace, or the great warriors of the army. So I presented myself as the simple shepherd-boy, the untutored child of nature. And of course in a sense all this was true. And it was also true that, as an artist, I had no idea – as true artists never have – of how I achieved my finest effects.

So I spoke in this manner and smiled. I watched myself do so, and I knew that the smile I gave her was one of my special smiles which I had used all my life to charm my mother and the ladies of her household.

"How modest," she said, and though I heard the irony in her voice, I knew that she was impressed, if only because she also recognised that I too was capable of irony, even while she was accepting me as someone naïve and unspoiled.

"Play to us," she said, "and then I'll be able to judge if you are speaking truth."

I hesitated. She slipped into the half-shadows and reclined on a couch, in receptive attitude. But still I held back. It would be easy to oblige and I could draw music from my harp which would charm her; but if I did so, that was how she would think of me: as a tame musician, which was not what I wished for. Yet I knew no other way to impress her, and I did not wish to appear sulky.

Then the curtain was torn aside and a young man strode into the room. He advanced upon me, laid his hands on my shoulders and embraced me, holding me fast and kissing me on both cheeks.

"I hope my sisters have been nice to you," he said. "We are so deeply in your debt that I trust they have been behaving better than they usually do."

"We have been perfectly charming, Jonathan," Michal said, "though in a more controlled fashion than you. I've just asked David to play to us."

"There's no need for that," he said. "He's not a professional entertainer, you know, and besides, I'm sure he's exhausted, aren't you, David?"

"I'm tired," I said, "but I'm quite happy to play, if that's what's wanted."

"No," he said, "you must come to supper with us instead."

He put his arm round my shoulder, leaning upon me, and led me through to another room where a table was laid.

That supper: I do not remember what we ate, or what we talked of, and not only because the wine was of a quality I had rarely tasted. In fact, I drank sparingly as has always been my custom. Nevertheless I was intoxicated by the charm and delight of the occasion. Jonathan had dismissed the slaves, and there were just the four of us. His zest took possession of the afternoon. It was no doubt an expression of relief that the dark boulder of the King's madness had been rolled away, and all felt as if they had been released from prison or even from the grave. I had never known such ease of company. I had never been received on such agreeable terms of equality, for at my father's table I was for ever caught between the desire of my brothers to snub me and subdue my pretensions and the eagerness of my mother and her women to spoil me. But here there was an easy give-and-take of conversation which encouraged even Michal to unbend.

If I had fallen headlong in love with Michal, I was now seduced by the charm of a family which offered something quite new to me. They were so fond of each other, and they willingly for that afternoon invited me to belong among them. I could have wept with happiness; instead I found myself laughing and talking as I had never talked before. I knew I was brilliant, warmed by the sun of Jonathan's encouragement and unforced affection.

I knew of his exploits of course. He was the darling of the tribe of Benjamin and indeed of the whole army. His courage, audacity, and enterprise in the wars were the talk of all Israel. I had felt a jealousy of his renown as it was brought to us in Bethlehem: he was only five years older than myself, had achieved so much while I herded sheep and made music. Now my jealousy was conquered by his charm. His beauty was unlike Michal's, being frank and open. The eagle's curve of his nose spoke of pride, but when he smiled, the smile travelled to his eyes, and his delight was manifest. He teased his sisters, but in the friendliest fashion. They had a habit of speaking sometimes in impromptu rhyme, and to my great pleasure, I was drawn into this conversation and held my own. If Jonathan had set himself to make me shine in the eyes of Michal, he could not have performed the task more wonderfully.

At last, unprompted, I said,

"Would you really like me to sing?"

They sent for my harp and I tuned it, and I sang a shepherd's song of unrequited love and longing. The music moved them. It silenced our merriment, and touched us with the essential sadness of life, of the brevity of youth and beauty. I sang of the mortality of all earthly joys, and we who were so joyful, knew a deeper joy in contemplating the inevitable hour when we would go into the dark.

In the morning Jonathan held me close and ruffled my hair as I pressed my face into his shoulder.

"How I wish, David, I could keep you with me."

The cold wind of his words stripped the young blossom from my tree.

"Listen, David," he said, his voice gentle and low, "listen carefully. The King has commanded that you return home. The memory of his madness revolts and distresses him. Your presence reminds him of it. It is an insult to his recovered strength, living testimony of those days and nights when he was less than a man. The sight of you, he says, is as a reproach to him. He is grateful for what you have done, and will load you with presents, but it is his wish that you remove yourself immediately from the court."

I fell – I am not ashamed to remember – to my knees. I clung to Jonathan's legs. I sobbed my grief and disappointment and the rage that consumed me. I railed against the injustice of the decree. I cried that if he truly loved me he would keep me by him. I clung to him and pleaded with his flesh, and as I felt his desire grow, knew hope. But then he held me off and spoke again.

"David, beloved, for that is what your name signifies, listen to me. I cannot oppose my father's will, for many reasons, and one is for your sake."

I would not listen, but his love compelled me.

"You are sixteen, only sixteen, caught in a trembling and

uncertain spring. In time you will return a man. I shall always love you, and you me, but not in this fashion."

"You are afraid of the priests," I said.

"No, David, it is because I love you that you must go. What has happened between us is good, not evil, but if you were to remain with me, you would come to feel it as evil, to learn shame and to despise yourself."

Then he took a cloth and dried my tears, and leaned forward, and kissed me, once, gently on the lips.

Abner provided an escort for me back to Bethlehem. There were two mules loaded with gifts from the King. I presented them to my father and mother, but it was long before I inquired as to their nature.

My parents were delighted by my achievement and the honour I had won, and I strove to conceal from them the misery which was tearing me apart.

Then I pondered Jonathan's words, and the strangeness of my own desires that drew me to both him and Michal, and for a time I was tormented, knowing that the priests condemned what Jonathan and I had done as abominable and contrary to nature.

But I had responded to Jonathan as naturally as a flower turns its face to the sun.

Now, in old age, I marvel at my own perplexity and at Jonathan's self-denial and self-knowledge. Forgetful for a moment of my infirmities, I gaze with longing on my ardent youth, and then call on Abishag to comfort me.

5

I have known much grief, but yet I wonder if there is any misery which can surpass that of a youth conscious of his powers and denied their exercise, who has been granted a glimpse of his promised land, and then found a curtain drawn to conceal the prospect. For two years I languished at home, a mere shepherd and goatherd. In the solitude of the night I cried out to the Lord:

"How long wilt Thou forget me, O Lord? For ever? How long wilt Thou hide Thy face from me, and deny me Thy favour? Consider and hear me, O Lord my God: lighten mine eyes lest I am compelled to sleep the sleep of death."

The formality of poetic language did little to staunch my wretchedness or ease my despair. What, I said to myself, can a poet do but make songs; yet my heart answered that I was more than a poet.

I knew temptation often in these months of longing, and there were girls in the village and in my father's house who would have been happy to satisfy my needs. Once I yielded, to a dark girl, a slave, born a Kenite; but after brief rhapsody and momentary release, shame took possession of me. It is strange to recall that feeling now, but my youth was by inclination chaste, virtuous, aspiring. The girl wept also, perhaps from happiness. Now I do not even recall her name.

My brothers remained with the army. The wars continued, ebbing to and fro, but most of the time only rumours came to us. Once a party of Philistine raiders passed through Bethlehem, in flight, scarcely drawing rein to loot. I watched the dust rise behind them as I crouched under an olive tree on the hill above, having driven my flock into a hollow where they were hidden.

Twice my brothers – Eliab, Abinadab and Shammah – came home when there was a lull in the fighting. They talked boastfully of their deeds, though Shammah confessed to me that in truth none had won great glory. He told me how Joab had advanced himself in Saul's favour, and must now be held to be the fourth man in the kingdom, behind Saul himself, Jonathan and Abner. When he spoke the name Jonathan, I was glad to be in the shadows that he might not see my face colour. I both desired and feared to hear his name. I drew my brothers on to mention him, and then looked away. But it was images of Michal that disturbed and excited my nights.

Eliab especially was warm in admiration of Joab. According to him, Jonathan's renown was the result not of his own qualities, but of the counsel and organising ability of Joab.

"Let's face it," he said, "Jonathan's flash, and Joab supplies the solid worth."

He was flushed with wine as he spoke and thumped the table. He was fat, complacent, and red-faced. It was of Eliab that I was thinking when I wrote that verse which is often quoted: "The fool hath said in his heart, there is no God."

He maintained also that Joab was worth two of Abner.

"If Abner wasn't Saul's cousin" – that was his constant refrain. I knew this also to be nonsense. I have never denied Joab's talents – indeed they have been necessary to me – but, as I shall show, he was inferior to Abner in all that matters in the sight of the Lord. Abner was a great gentleman (to use a word which I myself have coined as a means of encouraging the species of virtue I admire) while Joab, to be honest, was, is, and always will be, a shit.

"Jonathan's flash" . . . that was the sort of stupid military slang that Eliab delighted in. It made him feel that he was a man of the world, an insider. Poor Eliab. Much though I always disliked him, I find myself pitying him now. There is something pathetic about a man who so consistently overestimates his abilities and importance. He was always so certain he was right, and in truth rarely was.

I urged Shammah to persuade my father that I was now old enough to leave the flocks and take my place in the army. When he reported that Father said he must consult Eliab, my hopes were dashed. Besides, Father said, my mother was anxious that I should remain at home.

It was difficult, even with the advantage of the information relayed by my brothers, to understand the course of the war. In truth, as I see it now, it was for the most part a succession of confused skirmishes on the uncertain frontier between the Children of Israel and the Philistine tribes: raids on granaries and threshing-floors, burning of crops, driving off of herds, and the occasional attack on an ill-defended town. Saul and Jonathan achieved some success, enough anyway to provoke the Philistine kings into forming a union and, when I was in my eighteenth year, launching a great army against Israel, as if they were determined to make an end of Saul and reduce Israel to subjection. The word went round that the danger had never been greater, and then for a long time we heard nothing.

It seemed that the campaign had arrived at a decisive point, but that the commanders of both armies were afraid to make the first move. Word came from my brothers that they were stationed in the Valley of Elah with the Philistines drawn up on the hills opposite, and that they were running short of supplies. They begged my father to send them what he could, and I begged him to let me take charge of the expedition. He was loth to do so, but I prevailed, principally because there was no one else whom he could trust and he was too old to undertake the task himself. But he commanded me to return as soon as I had delivered the stores, so that I might let him know how my brothers fared. I do not think I am to be blamed for deciding secretly that I would do no such thing.

We travelled through the night, and arrived within sight of the camp as the morning mists were rising from the valley bottom. I was amazed, being ignorant of war, to see soldiers crouched over cooking-pots, oiling their bodies, dressing their armour, carrying buckets to the lines. I had had no true picture of military life, and it hadn't occurred to me that men have to carry out all the usual tasks of daily life even in the midst of a campaign. The stench from the latrines was revolting, by the way, and it is not too much to say that my first experience of camp life taught me the importance of attending to hygiene and supplies. Many an army has been destroyed by fever because the latrines were dug in an unsuitable place.

Only the night guard stood to arms. As I made my way through the camp, wondering if I should ever find my brothers in this confusion of men, trumpets sounded. I quickened my step, eager to see action, but someone told me that this was merely the signal for the relief of the night guard and their replacement by a new detachment.

"I'm afraid I don't understand," I said.

"Well," said a middle-aged soldier with a kindly expression, "it's no wonder if you should be confused if you're new to the camp. It's a strange position right enough. You see the stream down there. That's the bugger of it. We're both afraid to be the first to cross it, because the moment when you do so you're at a disadvantage. So we just sit and glower across the valley at one another, like two wildcats, and neither daring to move. Maybe we'll just have to see which side starves first. Are those supplies you have there, laddie, loaded on these asses?"

"Yes," I said, "but I have to deliver them to my brothers. If you're hungry though I can let you have a couple of loaves of bread, if you'll tell me where I can find my brothers, the sons of Jesse."

"The sons of Jesse?" He scratched his head. "Well," he said, "I don't rightly know. But I could do with some bread."

At that moment there came a blast of trumpets from across the valley, and a loud cheer which ran along all the ranks of the Philistines. Two men emerged into the sunlight, the first carrying a large shield before him, the second, even at that range, a huge figure. He advanced to the brow of the hill, and lifted a great horn to his mouth.

"The bugger," my new friend said. "Every bloody morning at the same bloody time."

"What is it? Who is it?"

"Listen and you'll know soon enough."

A silence had fallen on the camp, as if of shame. I recognised that immediately, though how I cannot tell. The Philistine gave vent to a mighty roar, magnified by means of the horn. I was not able to catch all the words, but the import was clear. He was challenging the army of Israel to produce a champion to do battle against him and decide the issue of the war.

He advanced farther towards us, all the time keeping his gaze fixed, and not seeming to notice how his shield-bearer moved in unison to guard him against any missile that might be thrown. He stepped forward till he was no more than fifty yards from the brook, and no more than that distance drawn in a straight line through the air between the two armies.

I looked at him closely. He had a helmet of brass on his head, and wore a coat of mail. His legs were protected by greaves of brass; he carried a long spear and a short thick sword was attached to his belt. And he was certainly very big. I had never seen so large a man. My brother Eliab was the biggest man I knew, taller even than the King, and this Philistine was head and shoulders taller than that, and big with it. Now he raised the horn again and bellowed, and this time I could distinguish the words.

"Are all the men of Israel cowards with the hearts of women that there is not one who dares accept my challenge?"

Then he laughed, and launched himself into obscenities, and threats of how he would despoil the body of anyone who set himself against him.

I was interested to hear him speak in this way, for it seemed to me that these last threats were intended to deter a challenger rather than to encourage one, and therefore that the huge Philistine might not be the hero he would have us think.

"Every bloody day," the soldier said, "and he'll pose there till the sun is past its height, laughing at us and cursing, till it fair makes you sick."

"And has no one accepted his challenge?" I asked.

"Look at him, laddie," said another soldier. "Look at the arms of him and the legs, look at his weapons, no bloody fear, thank you very much."

"They do say," a third said, "that the King has promised his daughter in marriage to any man who kills this Goliath, but I say, a dead man can't be a husband no matter the armful he's been promised."

"That's all nonsense," my first friend said. "The King's made no such promise, and for this reason: that he knows there's not a man in the army could defeat this Goliath, and he knows the effect that sending out a champion and then seeing him killed would have on the army."

"Aye," said the second soldier, "but what about the effect of not sending out one? What about that, eh?"

"But it's shameful," I said, "to let this brute insult us so."

"Oh shameful, is it," the third man said. "Well, speaking for myself, young fellow, I'd rather be ashamed than dead. Up to you of course if you think different. You go ahead and fight him if you like."

And he laughed. It was the mockery that did it.

"Right," I said, "I will. And I'll kill him. If no one else will defend the honour of Israel, then I will."

"The boy's mad."

"No, I'm not," I said. I mounted on to a rock to address the crowd which had now grown. "That man – Goliath is it you call him? – trusts in his brute strength and the terror he believes he can inspire. But I am not afraid, there is no terror in me, for I trust in the Lord of Hosts who brought Israel out of Egypt and delivered our forefathers from the hand of Pharaoh, as He will deliver me from the Philistine."

I had not thought about it, for I was indeed speaking as if the words did not belong to me, but were given me by the Lord, and so I spoke quietly with complete certainty, and my words and manner silenced the laughter, so that the soldiers surrendered themselves to me and laid aside their doubts. And my manner was, as I would have designed it had I been capable of thought, in stark contrast to the bullying boastfulness of the Philistine; and this too impressed those who heard me.

At that moment, I heard my name called, and turned and saw my brother Eliab. I do not think he had heard my speech, but I could see that he was furious to find me addressing the soldiers, and he snapped out:

"Why are you here? Why have you left your few sheep in the

hills? You've come to see the battle, haven't you? I know you, always poking your nose in where it's not wanted."

"So what have I done now?" I said. "And isn't there a good reason for what I'm about to do?"

I gestured across the valley at the Philistine, and to Eliab's fury, the men cheered and cried out, "Let's carry the boy to the King."

I had to wait, of course, outside Saul's tent while he was acquainted with the news that a volunteer had presented himself. I had no doubt that my offer would be accepted. This strikes me as strange now, for in Saul's position I would certainly have flattered such a young champion, but politely declined to let him get himself killed. Yet the possibility of refusal never occurred to me. My one anxiety was that I should not encounter Jonathan, not of course because I was not eager to see him, but because I knew that he would certainly intervene to try to persuade me, and, failing that, his father, that I should not engage Goliath. But I inquired of the guards as to his whereabouts, and was relieved to learn that he was commanding the right wing of the army and at present engaged in drilling his men.

At last I was admitted to Saul's presence. He gave no sign of recognition, but frowned, and for a moment I was reminded of his black mood of despair and madness. His cheeks were hollow and his eyes red-rimmed from lack of sleep or from weeping.

"So," he said. "So you want to fight this Goliath, and you're only a boy. It's . . ." and he paused, as if on the word "madness" which he would not care to utter, and substituted "foolishness".

"No, my lord king," I said. "It is not foolishness, for I trust in the Lord God of Israel. When I was only a child, my lord king, and watching over my father's flocks, there came a lion and another time a bear, and snatched a lamb. And though I was a child, I seized the lion and took the lamb out of its mouth, and then struck the lion and killed it, and on the other occasion I did the same to the bear, and I was able to do so because the Lord was with me. And He will defend me likewise against this uncircumcised Philistine who has made mock of the army of Israel and of my lord the King."

And then I knelt down before Saul, and took his hand, and kissed it, to show my loyalty and my confidence, and to suggest that all I sought from him was his blessing.

Still, he hesitated, and his hand twitched as if he would withdraw it, but I held fast and waited.

"Very well," he said, "it is foolishness, but . . ."

"My lord king, I said, "the Lord God of Hosts guards the simple-hearted who put their trust in Him and brings low the mighty man who trusts only in his own strength."

Saul sent for his armour-bearer, and ordered him to fetch me weapons and armour. Then he sat at his table and drank wine. (There are incidentally those who say that Saul was a drunkard, and that the deterioration in his character and capacity so evident in his later years was the consequence of his addiction to wine; but I do not think this is absolutely true.) I tried to imagine what he was thinking, whether he was regretting that he was no longer able to meet Goliath's challenge himself or that he had forbidden (as I subsequently discovered) Jonathan to match himself against the Philistine. I wondered if it was indeed the case that he had promised his daughter to anyone who conquered Goliath, and whether he would keep the promise, and if he was thinking of that. In truth, however, he was more probably brooding on the consequences of my challenge, for he told me to wait in an adjoining tent, and then I heard him summon Abner.

I put my ear to a join in the skins of which the tent was made, so that I might listen to their conversation.

Abner began by asking if it was true that a young man was about to take up Goliath's challenge, and spoke as if he thought it strange that Saul should have consented.

"I too thought it foolishness," the King replied, "and perhaps, though the boy is impressive in his way, that is the sensible view to take. But we can turn it to our advantage. In the first place, it lays Goliath open to ridicule. We have spoken several times, haven't we, of how the overthrow of a champion would demoralise the army, and for this reason we have not allowed anyone to go against the Philistine. But this is only a boy. If he is killed it is no great matter, no dishonour. Indeed the sight of a

youth being butchered by that great brute may inspire our men
with indignation. They will think him a hero and a martyr,
whereas . . . but no matter. I want you to give the order for
the men to stand at arms. Then the instant the thing is over,
when Goliath is parading in triumph, and the Philistines are
exulting, we shall launch an attack. It is the only way in which
we may hope to overcome the disadvantage of the ground which
has till now restrained us from doing so. We must break the
deadlock, before our army withers, and this is the best chance
we may get."

"Well," Abner said, "I'm sorry for the boy, but I agree
with you."

Saul laughed: "The boy talks with enthusiasm of the Lord God
of Hosts. Let him be a willing sacrifice to the Lord."

I cannot blame Saul for thinking as he did, but it was not an
encouraging conversation to overhear, though later I admired
the acuity with which Saul grasped that a chance of victory had
been given to him, and how to achieve it.

Then I was summoned back to the royal tent, which Abner
had left. Saul told me that a tent had been assigned me, and
that my armour was waiting for me there. He said he would
see me again before I marched against the Philistine, whom, as
I emerged from his tent, I could still see parading and preening
himself on the hill opposite.

"There is not long to lose," Saul said, "if you are to fight
today."

My attendants were respectful, as if in awe of the courage I was
displaying. The armour was magnificent. I dressed myself in a
golden tunic of rich cloth which Saul had also sent, and I allowed
the slaves to deck me in armour, and the jewelled brass helmet,
and I felt myself to be a mighty warrior, and knew myself to look
so splendid that I wished when I returned to present myself to
the King that Michal might be there to see me.

But when I was with Saul again, I removed the armour and
the fine clothes and stood before him in a simple rough tunic,
with a leather belt round my waist and my feet bare.

For I said to him: "I have not tested this armour and I
am not accustomed to these weapons. I shall fight and slay

Goliath in my own manner, and with the simple weapons of the hills."

I requested, however, that the armour and fine clothes should be taken back to the tent Saul had assigned to me, for I regarded them as a gift of which I was about to prove myself worthy.

Then I left the King and walked, very slowly, as one walks who is at ease, through the camp, with my sling round my neck, and looking neither to right nor to left, but savouring the murmurs of appreciation, the cries of "Good fortune", that came to me from every side. I got beyond the front lines and descended to the brook, and a deep silence fell behind me. I kept my eyes lowered and did not look towards Goliath.

At the brook I knelt down and prayed to the Lord, and then chose five smooth stones from the water, and put them in my shepherd's scrip, and with my staff in my hand crossed over the water, and advanced against the Philistine. As I did so, I raised my head and looked at him and smiled, for I knew that this would enrage him.

There was silence from both camps, and Goliath beat his breast and roared:

"Am I a dog that you come to me with a staff in your hand?"

Then he cursed me by his gods: Dagon with his fish-head, Baal-zebub, the Lord of Flies, and Atargatis, the she-devil.

"Come on," he yelled, "and I shall deliver your flesh to the fowls of the air."

"Not so," I said, "you have your spear and your sword, but I come to you in the name of the Lord God of Israel, who has sworn to deliver you into my hand. And I shall cut off your head and set it up to be a trophy and a witness to the power of the Lord God of Hosts. For the battle is the Lord's and He has delivered you to me."

As I expected, this defiance infuriated the brute and he lumbered towards me. But I skipped away, keeping out of range and continuing to taunt him. This went on for some time, and, when necessary, I crossed back over the brook where he did not dare to follow, for he would there find himself among the front lines of our army. I would then run along the bank and cross over again, forcing him to turn and give chase. And all the time he grew hotter and more short of breath but continued to curse as his fury grew. I was deliberately making him look foolish for I realised there were two things necessary for success: first, I must get him to throw his spear, so that he could only engage me at close quarters where I had no intention of finding myself; second, I had to detach him from his shield-bearer who, however, being an experienced soldier, was proving skilful at keeping a guard over his master.

So I let him approach me more closely as I hovered on the edge of the stream. I paused as if out of breath, and with a roar of triumph, he hurled his javelin. Since I was ready for it, I skipped aside, and it buried itself in the ground on the Israelite side of the brook. I scrambled up the hillside, on a diagonal, running towards the Philistine army as if overcome by sudden panic. I made to stumble and threw myself on the ground. I got uncertainly to my feet, and felt my knee, rubbing it, to suggest that I was injured. Looking back over my shoulder, I hobbled a few yards, and turned and faced him, letting my mouth fall open. I even uttered a hopeless sob, and he thrust his shield-bearer aside, and raising his huge sword in both hands above his head, charged towards me, roaring his wrath and triumph. I slipped a stone from the satchel into my sling, and let it fly. It caught him just below the helmet, full in the face, and he fell to the ground. I looked up. His shield-bearer stood amazed, then turned, and fled towards his lines. I advanced on Goliath. He lay on his back, the stone buried in his forehead. I touched him with my foot, and the body did not stir. I took the sword from the rocks where it had fallen, and hacked at his neck. It was a harder job than I would have imagined, but at last it was done. I tucked his helmet under my arm, and holding the bloody thing by the hair, descended the hill. At that very instant I was all but swept aside by our own soldiers who with yells of exultation had crossed the stream and were charging up the hill against the Philistine army. I did not look to see the result, but resumed my descent, crossed the brook, and mounted the hill towards Saul's tent.

Silence surrounded me. I looked back across the valley and saw the Philistines in flight.

6

Of course Saul did not give me Michal. Perhaps the story that he had promised her to the man who would slay Goliath had no foundation, but was one of those rumours that flit so freely through camps. (Soldiers are as addicted to rumour as village-women.) Yet I do not think so. More probably Saul had indeed, in a moment of anxiety, made such an offer, which he now found it convenient to forget, may indeed actually have forgotten. His grasp on reality was weakening, something which no one who loved or admired him could observe without pain.

There was nobody to whom I could confess my desire for Michal, and though I was rewarded for my victory over Goliath by evidence of the King's favour, it would have been thought presumptuous of me to aspire to the hand of his daughter. So I was compelled to wait on events, trusting that the Lord would so compass them that my patience would be rewarded.

I was careful not to seem boastful or arrogant. I knew that my position was precarious. There were many ready to ascribe my triumph to good fortune, and many more who were jealous that one so young should have acquired such distinction. To my surprise, Joab did not appear to be among them. I had overleapt him, but he courted my favour, and showed me none of the studied indifference, approaching contempt, with which he had hitherto regarded me. I was not however so naïve as to be completely deceived by this; I was on the other hand encouraged, for I knew Joab to be intensely ambitious and I saw that his manner to me indicated that he was confident my star was rising. The truth is that Joab has always been a man who cared more for the reality of power than for its semblance. He knew that he lacked the magnetism which a man must have to rise to the first place in the kingdom; he knew also that he could never challenge the dominance of the tribe of Benjamin while Saul lived (for the King in his fearful melancholy was loth to trust any but his immediate family and kinsmen). Besides, Joab hated Jonathan and was jealous of Abner; he knew that neither favoured him. So his attachment to me was a matter of interest, not affection.

How different from Jonathan! On the evening of the day I killed Goliath, when I was in my tent, admiring the gorgeous armour which I had not used, Jonathan came to me, straight from the battlefield where he had added to his glory. His face shone with exultation and his thighs were streaked with grime and dried blood, and when he embraced me, there was the sweat of battle in the warmth of his body. For a long time we did not speak, but held each other close and wrestled with the ardour of youth that seeks release after the terrors and perils of the battlefield. By our deeds that day we were drained of morality, of responsibility, even of will, and we slaked our needs in each other's body, affirming the life which might have been stripped from us, as the red leaves of autumn are torn from the tree. It was as if, quivering together with hot young limbs entangled, we found in the intimate darkness of the goat-skinned tent an equivalent of the mental passion we had expended in the agony of battle. When we were done, we held each other at arm's length and sought each other's soul in each other's eyes. We knew neither guilt nor shame, though the act is condemned as abomination, for what we had done seemed to us both not only natural but necessary.

Then at last Jonathan spoke, but I cannot bring myself to write the words he uttered, for to do so would give them a significance quite different from that which they have in my heart. Words of love are for lovers only, and, no matter how a poet writes, the words he speaks to his beloved are usually banalities. With women, in my considerable experience, banalities serve best, and any attempt to go beyond them results in absurdity or misunderstanding.

There is never such a thing as equality in love. There is always one lover who kisses and the other who offers cheek or lips; and this is so whatever form the act of congress itself may take. The balance may shift. The adored may become the adorer, at which point – except perhaps for a brief moment of ecstasy – the first adorer slips into the position of being the adored. Our situation was in no way equal, for Jonathan was the King's son and I was a raw youth. Nevertheless it was he who urged and I who consented, so that in the island moments of passion, the balance of inequality that prevailed beyond the tent was tipped the other way. The high-minded virtue that had caused Jonathan to deny himself what he most dearly desired, for two years, had served only to deepen and enrich his passion, which I, starved of joy by my own chastity and excluded from the love I hungered for, now eagerly satisfied, feeding an appetite which I could not prevent.

And Jonathan was tender to me. That was a great gift. He cared for my reputation, taking pains to ensure that our liaison remained hidden from the prying eyes of the camp, or at worst conjectural. Though he never hesitated to advance me before men, in the King's council and in the army, he restrained himself from public displays of affection, and took care to commend my intellect rather than my person. He even schooled himself to abstain from the pleasure of looking at me in such a way as might arouse the suspicions of even the best-disposed towards me, and he denied himself that especial pleasure, with which the secret lover so easily and infallibly betrays his passion: the too-frequent introduction of the loved one's name in conversation. This was the more remarkable, and sure evidence to me of the depth and virtue of his love, since he was by nature frank and open, not given to reticence or duplicity.

I cannot withhold some credit from myself for the success with which we concealed the nature of our love. It could not have been kept secret had I been only a pretty boy, of no consequence in other matters. (But then Jonathan would not have loved such a boy.) As it was, a combination of my own achievement and capacity, and the respect which this won me, ensured that I was soon taking a prominent part in the organisation of the army. You must understand that Israel was then a young state, free from the trammels of ceremony which are to be found in long-established polities, and so, since our organisation was rudimentary or even experimental, opportunities were given to the young and inventive which would have been denied them in other circumstances. (I observe by the way that young Solomon, old though not wise beyond his years, is inclined to admire formality in structures and methods of doing business, which will certainly restrict the development of talents like mine in the kingdom as he will direct it. That will be Israel's loss, but nothing I say will influence that young man who is so eager for me to depart the scene.)

It was clear that the victory at Elah which my defeat of Goliath had made possible had secured Israel only temporary relief. The Philistines had been driven out of the low hill-country of Shephelah, but Saul had not ventured to pursue them into the plain and continue the campaign there. So they had retired comfortably into their cities of Gath, Askelon and Zimlag, ready to renew war when it suited them. There could be no security for Israel till the Philistines had been subdued.

That was a task which seemed beyond us, and from which most people, even Saul, shrank. The King's doubts are to be excused. He had spent so many years in intermittent to-and-fro warfare with the Philistines that he had ceased to believe – if indeed he had ever believed – in the possibility of a final victory. For him war with Philistia was part of life, as natural as the seasons, and life without it was as inconceivable as life without the seasons. So easy is it for the set of a man's mind to become fixed.

There were naturally good reasons for this condition of mind, however diseased it might seem to me. I was ready to admit them. For one thing, the Philistines were, man for man, better fighters than the Israelites, braver and stronger in physique. Curiously, when I mentioned this, to me, incontrovertible fact, there was an uproar, coming ironically from those who believed that war with the Philistines could never be brought to a successful conclusion, while I, who thought it could, was quite prepared to admit this unpleasant reality. The uproar in the council chamber was opportunely and characteristically quelled by Jonathan, remarking with a smile:

"It is no wonder David thinks as he does, for Goliath was indubitably of superior physique to him, and yet suffered total defeat. I imagine David is going to tell us that we are superior in one important respect . . ."

"And what's that?" Saul said, scowling.

"Intelligence, Father."

I was pleased to see Achitophel, by some way the cleverest civilian member of the council, smile.

Jonathan, I said, had anticipated me. We were, in my opinion, superior in intelligence. I paused there to permit a degree of self-satisfaction to be entertained. The pause was fortunate, for it enabled me to stop myself from adding that it was not much good being superior in intelligence if we refrained from applying it to the question. All my life I have had to take great care not to allow myself to seem cleverer than those I am dealing with, and perhaps one of the most useful things Jonathan ever did for me was to persuade me to try to disguise my intellectual superiority in vague and civil phrases. One reason, incidentally, why we Israelites are so disliked and distrusted by our neighbours is that so many of us allow them to see that we know them to be our intellectual, as well as moral, inferiors.

Bearing this in mind, having caught a quick frown on Jonathan's face, which I interpreted correctly as a warning, I embarked, as we had agreed, on an analysis of the military disparity between the Philistines and ourselves. Their great advantage lay in their development of the war-chariot, combining mobility with formidable power of destruction. In a formal battle in open country, this was too much for our conventional infantry armed with javelins, spears and short swords, for the archers carried in the chariots could do enormous damage while themselves out of range of our javelins, and then, when our lines had been weakened, the onslaught of the chariots themselves too often proved irresistible. We found it hard to compete, for Israel was not horse-rearing country, though if we could seize and occupy a stretch of the coastal plain, things would be different in that respect. Meanwhile it seemed to me we must try to develop forces which were even more mobile than the chariots, light-armed slingers and bowmen. I pointed out that a foot-soldier could wield a more powerful bow than the chariot archers. We could defeat the Philistines in irregular warfare, and even in pitched battles if we chose our ground carefully – and here I paid tribute to the astuteness of Saul's selection of the Vale of Elah, terrain in which the Philistines had found their chariots of little use. But, I added, if we were to carry the war into the plain we not only had to improve our mobility, but train our spearmen – now better protected by the slingers and bowmen – to withstand the chariot charge. I had some ideas on that too, I remarked, but perhaps I had said enough for the time being.

A general discussion ensued, in which my ideas came under attack from the traditionalists. Jonathan intervened only to question some of their assumptions, but refrained, as we had agreed, from openly supporting my argument. Abner for a long time kept silent. Saul himself appeared distracted, crumbling bread between his fingers till the crumbs were grey, and then clapping his hands for a slave whom he sent for wine. He drank two cups quickly and sat with a full cup in his right hand, while the fingers of his left hand resumed their crumbling motion. It was impossible to tell whether the discussion bored him, whether he resented my implicit criticism of his conduct of affairs – even though I had sugared it with praise – whether he was pondering the matters I had raised, or whether he had abstracted himself and drifted into that private world which his mind so often now seemed to inhabit.

Then Achitophel raised a hand, and Abner, who without a word had taken over control of the meeting as Saul insensibly resigned it, called on him to speak. I don't remember just what he said, but his manner remains clear: the soft sibilant insinuating tone, the suggestion that it was unpardonable of him to speak, but that since he was committing such a solecism, he must express his profound appreciation of our willingness to listen. In this way, with deep apologies for his foolhardiness, he carried the meeting – as he usually did.

Achitophel was an oddity. Neither priest nor soldier, he had no evident status, could point to no achievement, and yet, where things were decided, there was Achitophel, forming the decision. One day perhaps there will be some term that adequately describes such as Achitophel; I feel sure that he represents a type of the future. If the society which I have worked to create becomes established – and to do justice to Solomon, he, alone of my sons, understands that I have been trying to form a nation out of tribes, and to create something unprecedented, which indeed I find it impossible to name, since the words for what does not yet exist are naturally not to be found in our language, and indeed I myself have only a glimmering of what I intend – if, as I say – but I grow lost in the parentheses of old age – such a society comes into being, there may be many Achitophels. Perhaps the explication of the law will no longer be a matter reserved to the priests, but for a whole class of Achitophels. I admire him despite everything.

In those days of which I am now writing I had reason to be grateful to him. He was an adherent of Jonathan, for he saw that Saul's star was declining, and ambition led him to attach himself to my friend. He may even have been his confidant in the most intimate matters. I suspected as much from the calculating way he regarded me. Of course he looked at everyone with calculation, but there was something tender and watchful in his manner towards me which I found unsettling because it spoke of knowledge which I would from choice have denied him. That said, being a partisan of Jonathan, he was well inclined towards me. The upshot of his speech now was that I had my way. I was assigned the task of training the new army of Israel and organising its equipment and the tactics it would employ in battle.

The months that followed were full of delight. I worked long hours and did not grudge them. I was blessed with the zest of youth and I felt my power. There are few greater pleasures in life than exercising one's talents to the full, and few greater than taking a body of raw recruits and moulding them into a fighting force.

I took Joab as my lieutenant. (One should never allow personal feelings to influence the choice of subordinates. Solomon, it occurs to me, will be a good picker of men because he is incapable of liking anyone.) Joab did the job excellently, as I knew he would; you could give him an order and be certain that it would be carried out. He had not yet learned to overestimate his capacity. His judgement in military matters was admirable, and it was only in those that I wished to engage him.

We soon achieved results. Our troops, trained to a high level of physical fitness, and supremely confident of their abilities – as soldiers usually are when they trust their commanders – began to inflict a succession of defeats on the Philistines, who were amazed to find that Israelite forces now moved faster than they did, and continually caught them by surprise.

One other thing: though I naturally drew my élite troops from my own tribe of Judah, my brother Shammah proving an excellent officer, I was careful to involve members of as many of the twelve tribes as possible. There was good military reason for this; we were not so numerous that we could afford to neglect any human resources. But I also thought that it might serve me well in the future if I built up a store of credit with the northern tribes.

I became a popular figure. Nothing displayed the nobility of Jonathan's character more clearly than his complete lack of resentment at my success. It was not the same with Saul. When he heard that there was a popular song which declared that "Saul has slain his thousands, but David his tens of thousands", there were many to advise him that I was becoming a rival, and he was not averse to entertaining the suspicion himself. It was nonsense. I was still only twenty when girls could be heard singing that song as they drew water from the wells at twilight.

But poor Saul more and more dwelled in a twilight world himself.

7

How lovely were the mornings when the Lord sang the beauty of His creation! On one such day, with the dew still glistening and a pale crescent of moon still visible on the hilltops, themselves turned pink and golden by the rising sun, I returned from a night exercise – for I had determined that my troops should be as formidable and certain in the darkness as in the daylight – glowing with the health and happiness that mimic war affords. The day was crowned with goodness and the paths I trod promised me abundance. The pastures were clothed with flocks and the little hills rejoiced on every side.

I bathed in a pool encircled by willows, and my servant laid out clean garments for me.

"Master," he called, "my lord, there are women approaching."

So I dressed hurriedly, and emerged from the grove to encounter Michal in the company of her waiting-women.

I felt myself flush as if I had been a raw youth and not the man I had become.

"So you have discovered my secret pool," she said, and stretched our her hand to touch my wet hair.

"I did not know."

"What a great man you have become, no longer the poor musician employed to distract my father."

Her words reduced me to that status, and deprived me of speech.

"Why have you avoided me since you became so great a man? Does my brother require your constant attendance?"

"My lord Jonathan has been very kind."

"But of course," she said, "and being so great a warrior you now have no time for anything but war. Or so they tell me."

My eyes devoured her. She did not resent their scrutiny, fell indeed into an attitude that invited it more intensely. The waiting-women drew back at a sign from her, and we were left alone in the grove. She put her hands to cover her breasts which showed above the low neck of her gown, and then, with a smile, lowered her arms.

"If I have avoided you," I said, "it is because I cannot look upon you without desiring you."

With these words I surrendered myself to her power. If she had not been Saul's daughter . . . but then would I have felt as I did if she had not been? She held out those pale thin hands which had never been required to work.

"Here I am."

"Saul would kill me," I said.

She laughed.

"Of course he would. Here I am."

Her laughter emboldened me.

"I want you as my lover," I said, "but also as my wife."

"Oh David," she said. "I am so bored. Speak to my father."

"And if I do? If I dare to?"

"Dare to? Aren't you the boy who killed a wolf and a bear and a Philistine giant? And you hesitate to speak a word?"

I was in bed with Jonathan when I told him I wanted to marry his sister.

"You don't need to tell me that," he said, and kissed me.

He assured me he would help, but then told me what I knew and feared to hear him say: that Saul would be furious because his feelings for me were so complicated.

"One day he tells me to beware of you, that your ambition is naked and that you will destroy me. Then he speaks of you fondly, as if you, not I, were his favourite child."

"Yes," I said, "he wants to kill me, but he would weep over my corpse."

"David," Jonathan said, "you don't need to pretend to me.

Priests blab. I know all about the visit that Samuel paid to your father's house, and what happened then."

"Does Saul?"

"David, David, do you think, if he did, you would be here to ask that question? There are matters people dare not tell the king."

"But you know, and I am."

He smiled, and ran his finger along the line of my jaw.

"Let us just say I can't help myself," he said. "Alternatively, that I was never greatly impressed by Samuel. Alternatively, that I believe that if it is written it is written. Alternatively, that I can deny you nothing. I shall speak to my father."

"Michal," I said, "knows about us."

"My sister is very clever."

"I would much rather," I said, "I was not in love with her."

"Then you are, utterly," he said.

That was how it started. Jonathan was to persuade his father. It didn't make sense to me then, but I trusted him to do his best. That's strange, isn't it? I mean, why should he? If he succeeded, he lost me. That was the last time we made love actually. He didn't stop loving me, sometimes I thought he loved me more than ever, but . . . I didn't understand it, and in a way I don't yet. I've never loved anyone like that, not even Michal. Perhaps especially not Michal. I've tried to love the Lord that way – His will, not mine – but I don't think I've succeeded. Like Samuel, I hate to say this, but like Samuel, most of my life, I have had no difficulty in persuading myself that my will is, by a stroke of great good fortune, the Almighty's. And it may have been. I can't be sure it wasn't. The successes I've had, my recoveries from the depths, they make me believe, at the right moment, that I am indeed the Chosen of the Lord, here to enact His will. Which I can only interpret by following my own.

Now, in the long watches of the night, I am afraid: of dying, of not dying. I listen to the easy breathing of Abishag the Shunnamite girl, and I want to stick knives into her because she will be alive when I no longer am. And yet I cry out for rest.

I have come to hate everybody, that's the trouble. Except, oddly, Abishag, who does bring me some comfort. I only want to stick knives into her because she is the one who is here. Instead, I stroke her tawny flanks with my withered hand, and pretend to myself that the tenderness she shows me comes from the heart.

It doesn't. It couldn't.

In the long watches reproaches rise like avenging ghosts. Only Jonathan has nothing with which to reproach me because I came as close to honesty with him as is possible for one of my secretive nature.

There was one night when, returning from a raid against the Philistines, the triumph of victory drained from us, to be succeeded by a shame that neither of us could account for. We had slain some dozen of the infidel, and known joy as we surveyed their corpses. Yet that evening, Jonathan said, in a murmur so that only I might hear, "But they were men, you know, framed as we are." It was as well he spoke in a whisper; Joab for instance would have regarded his words as a sort of treason. But I understood him, and pressed his cold hand in the damp night.

I was not well. My body ached with headache and fever, the consequences or blood brother of a sharp attack of dysentery which had troubled me on our march, and left me faint and querulous. As ever, this disease which plagues soldiers on the move left me tired and despondent.

At that moment a quarrel broke out among the men. Our patrol – for it had been little more – was composed almost equally of Jonathan's men and the light infantry troops whom I had been training. The cause of the quarrel was never established. There came a shriek, a cry of rage, and then sobbing. We ran to investigate, my bowels aching with the rapidity of movement. Someone lit a lantern. Then we saw Nehemiah, one of Jonathan's sergeants, with his throat cut. My man, Azreel, stood with a bloody knife in his hand, guilt manifest, but an expression of bewilderment on his face, as if the knife had acted of its own accord, without intent. There was nothing for it. My head was aching with fever, and I could scarcely think. Joab, pushing forward, gave the order. The wretched Azreel was surrendered to Jonathan's troopers. Nehemiah's brother took the knife from his guilty hand and pressed its point against his neck. I closed my eyes. Jonathan spoke. "Not like that," he said. What did he mean? "This is not a blood feud," he said. "It must not be allowed to become that. Azreel must stand trial formally."

"It is the Law of Moses," cried out Nehemiah's brother. "Blood for blood, an eye for an eye."

"Not like that," Jonathan said again. "David," he said, "you are his commanding officer . . ."

My mouth was dry, clamouring to vomit. Horror rose before me. I would fain have thrown myself on the ground and whimpered. But eyes were upon me. I spoke, and my voice was like a broken reed. I told Azreel he must die, but at the hands of his own commander. I took the knife with which he had killed Nehemiah from the offended brother, and with a trembling hand, under the pale moon, thrust it into Azreel's neck. His blood spurted over me. He fell to his knees spitting more blood. I knelt beside him. He was dying by inches. I put my arms round him, drawing him still lower and covering his head with my cloak. I drew out the knife and stabbed again and cradled him in my arms as his lifeblood flowed over the sand towards the rocks.

In the morning the men looked at me with dull hostility. I told them to dig a grave for Azreel.

8

It was Joab who brought me the news of the rumours that encircled me.

When he first broached the matter I was afraid, thinking that his reports might refer to my relations with Jonathan: "an abomination" in the eyes of the priests, though for many of them to speak thus was hypocrisy. But, no, it was rather my desire for Michal that had become the talk of the court; equally condemned as presumption.

"Someone," Joab said, "will tell the King, and then . . ."

I recognised fear in his eyes; he was wondering whether he could separate himself from my fate, or whether he was too closely identified with me.

"Why should King Saul object?" I said. "He is king, but before he was that, he was as humbly born as I, more so indeed, for Jesse is a man richer in flocks than ever Kish was with his miserable lost asses . . ."

I spoke rashly, but I did so to stimulate Joab, and force him to declare himself. But Joab was canny, and shifted ground.

"There are rumours also," he said, "concerning the visit Samuel made to your father's house."

"And do you believe them?"

"I am here," he said, "and I have talked with your brothers."

"In that case, I have nothing to fear. You know what Samuel did, you know that he named me the Chosen of the Lord, and anointed me with holy oil. Can the Lord's purpose be prevented? What has the Chosen of the Lord to fear from Saul, whom the Lord of Hosts has rejected?"

I spoke thus to bind Joab to me, but I did not feel the confidence that I expressed. Certainly there were moments when I believed myself inviolable, a being set apart to fulfil the purpose of the Lord; but there were also times when it seemed to me that I was no more than the instrument of an old man's spite.

It was soon after this that, as we had agreed, Jonathan broached the matter of my marriage to his father. No doubt he chose his moment carefully, when Saul was in one of his now rare moods of sunshine and euphoria. At any rate he extracted a promise, though Saul also set a condition: I might marry Michal if I brought the King the foreskins of a hundred Philistines. This I naturally accomplished. Joab muttered that Saul had no doubt hoped that I would be killed in the enterprise; but I do not believe this. I had after all acquired a considerable reputation as a slayer of Philistines, and in fact returned with near double the number of required foreskins. Our marriage, and my first ambition, were therefore achieved.

Michal still visits me in dreams, or in the half-sleep which is all my portion now; but I find it difficult to write of her. There is a certain shame attached. She desired me, as I did her; and yet in our love-making I experienced a distance between us which I have never known with another woman. It was as if a part of her remained removed, watching us, and engaged in assessment. Even in moments of culminating passion, when her legs were wrapped round me, and we rocked in common ardour, I sensed this detachment, this refusal ever to surrender her whole being to me. And yet she protested her love as we lay damp together, and often wept tears which, she assured me in soft murmurs, were of joy. Her skin was soft as rose-petals and her kisses sweet as honey. I knew infinite delight, and yet my longing was never appeased.

Saul fell again to brooding, then to a deep melancholy, then to silence, then to fearful and angry looks, then to despair made terrible by the imminence of violence. Abner begged me to sing to him again, to repeat the magic I had formerly worked.

I hesitated.

When I came to Saul before, I thought, I was an unknown boy, with a beautiful voice. He knew nothing of me and I might have been a spirit sent to minister to him by the Lord. That experience cannot be repeated. No man can bathe in the same river twice, for the river has changed, and the first water has run towards the sea. Now Saul knows me well, and his feelings towards me are confused. One day he is rich in words of love; the next he fixes me with a look of loathing.

But I consulted Jonathan and Michal, and though she would not at first answer, Jonathan begged me to make the attempt. Michal then said,

"Are there no other bards in Israel that you must demean yourself?"

I felt her contempt, but feeling it, I saw that it was the Lord's will that I should humble myself and sing to Saul.

The King crouched in the corner of a darkened room, more terrible than on the first occasion, because now I knew him and could fathom better the nature of the evil possession in which he was held. He darted a glance at me in which even in the dim light I read hatred and malignancy; and his fingers picked at each other, and had worn the skin raw and bleeding.

I sang first in a low voice, a lullaby such as mothers use to calm their children. Then I crooned an old ballad which had delighted Saul as he sat feasting, for it spoke of the glory of his courage in the bright morning of Israel. I sang his praises and he did not stir. Then remembering my earlier attempt, I broke into the praise of the Lord my shepherd. The King's eyelids twitched, and when I reached the verse which tells of the soul's journey through the dark vale of death, he rose unsteadily to his feet. For a moment he stood swaying as if understanding broke in on him, and in that moment I believed I was working the same magic as before. But then he lurched towards a corner of the room, where spears were stacked against the wall – I later learned that he had defied all attempts to remove them. He seized one, and drew his arm back. I leapt aside as the spear struck the wall behind me, and hung quivering there, as I slipped through the curtains and to safety.

"So you failed," Michal said.

"I failed. He knew it was me, and he wanted to kill me. Yes, I failed."

We clung together in misery, and then it was as if the knowledge of my failure had broken the dam of her reserve, for she gave herself utterly to me; and our fear and wretchedness were translated into bliss such as neither of us had ever known.

Our joy was the more intense because I knew it could not last. Perhaps Michal felt this also, though she said nothing to that effect. It was ever her way to keep silence. Only when she was angered would she speak her mind. Distrustful of good fortune, she felt that happiness was something to be concealed, lest it be snatched from her. Or so I now believe; then I was puzzled and made uneasy by her reticence. She had this ability always to make me feel that I had failed her. Even that night, after Saul's attempt on my life, when she turned away to sleep, my hand resting between her thighs, she seemed to be slipping from me, who had a moment earlier had the illusion of possessing her entirely.

In the morning I rose apprehensively. Hourly, I expected a guard to come and arrest me. When I ventured out, I caught fear in men's eyes. Word of the King's attempt had spread; they did not know when they gazed on me whether to salute the captain whom the Philistines feared, or to avert their eyes from a wretch whom the King had condemned.

Jonathan alone was unaltered.

He was unaltered because he did not understand.

"Dear boy," he said, "my poor father was out of his mind. That's all there is to it. When he recovers . . ."

"If he recovers . . ."

"Until he recovers he can give no order which will not first be referred to Abner or myself, both of whom love you. When he recovers, he will repent of this act, which in his right mind he will condemn even as I do."

I wished I could share his confidence. Instead I argued with him. I told him that Saul's madness was different now, more deep-seated. I said that Saul's fear and resentment of me had eaten into his nature; that he could never love me again; that he saw me now as the instrument of Samuel's vengeance.

"I do not want to flee into exile," I said. "I do not want to abandon Michal. I do not want to be an outlaw. But . . ."

We left that "but" hanging in the air. Jonathan undertook to try to restore the situation. I did not believe this possible, and took my leave.

"Whatever happens," Jonathan said, "nothing can divide you and me. I shall care for you and yours, and you for me and mine."

"Whatever happens," I replied; and we embraced.

Yet I delayed. I could not bring myself to accept what I knew to be true: that everything for which I had striven was about to be taken from me. I was afraid, also, afraid of returning to the loneliness I had known as a boy. I begged Michal to make ready to accompany me. She answered that her love was great, but that she could not see herself as a fugitive in the wilderness.

"Very well," I said, "I shall stay here and die. The thought of losing you is worse than the thought of losing my life."

"Rhetoric," she said. "If you lose your life, you lose me anyway."

Saul struggled back from the darkness. He observed my absence from his table. Jonathan told him that I had gone to Bethlehem for a family celebration and sacrifice. For a moment – I am told – Saul said nothing, but crumbled the bread between his torn fingers. Then he cursed Jonathan for a fool, a bastard, and a traitor.

"David has bewitched you," he shouted. "You put your lust for your catamite above your loyalty to your father."

Jonathan could not speak. Even Abner hesitated to come between the King and his anger.

"The boy must die," Saul said.

"He has done nothing to deserve death," Jonathan protested. Or so it is reported; I do not know. I would like to believe he spoke up for me, but Saul was dreadful in his mad anger, and even Jonathan may not have dared to oppose him.

*   *   *

Saul sent guards to Bethlehem to arrest me. I took my leave of Michal and fled into the night. I wept as we parted, but she urged me to make speed.

9

I watched the dawn break from a cave in the bare rocks, and scoured the plain for signs of pursuit. I prayed to the Lord, calling to Him to be mindful of my fidelity and of how I had never served any other god, of how my faith had never faltered in the days of my prosperity, and of how I trusted in Him still in my distress. And then I slept.

When I woke the sun was lipping the cave. I ran my hands the length of my thighs, pressed them together, and longed for Michal. My desire was intense, but when it passed, I found relief in my solitude. The sun rose to its zenith, baking the brown earth and gilding the rocks. I gazed into the wide and empty plain. A hawk hovered overhead, but there was no sound to break the midday silence. There came on me a sensation of a brooding peace as the world brimmed with the essential light of the Lord's glory.

I rested my back against the warm rock and waited. The hawk swooped, but rose again, its claws empty, having missed its prey. I watched it hover in the unbroken quiet of the windless day. I raised the goatskin to my lips and drank of the wine and water, and then slept again.

Towards evening I descended the hillside, my feet slipping on the scree. Throughout the day I had let my mind lie fallow; action, I have ever believed, is not best determined by thought. I moved with a light carefulness along the little ridge of the foothills, until, rounding a corner, I saw light in the valley below. And then I paused again, and waited, till the cloak of night had fallen and the torches had been extinguished. Below me, as I knew, lay Nob, a settlement of priests, governed by Abimelech, grandson of Eli, Samuel's master. I knew him for one who had stood with Samuel against Saul; yet I dared not confess that I myself was a fugitive from the King, lest Abimelech or some of the other priests might seize the opportunity to find favour with the King by apprehending me. Moreover, I suspected that fear might deter them from aiding one whom the King had condemned.

Abimelech himself advanced to meet me, and when he heard who I was, showed alarm. I told him that I was engaged on a secret mission on Saul's behalf, and that it was imperative that none should learn of my visit. He looked at me doubtfully, and I could see that he wondered at my arrival alone and unheralded. I said I had arranged to meet my men at a secret place nearby, and had come in search of provisions.

"We have no common bread, only holy bread," Abimelech said.

"Let me then have five loaves of the last week's shew-bread," I said.

"Are you and your men clean or unclean? For, as you know, the shew-bread may only be given to those who have kept themselves from women."

"Truly," I said, "women have been kept from us for three days."

Abimelech then, though still nervous, commanded that the bread should be fetched, and this was done by a man I recognised, Doeg, an Edomite, a villainous-looking fellow with a cast in his eye, who had formerly served in Saul's household.

I stowed the bread in my knapsack, and took my departure. Abimelech was eager to see me gone, and I had no desire to delay.

"The King," I said, "will be grateful to you for the help you have given me"; and so I disappeared into the night.

Now at last I admitted to myself where I was going. I have often wondered at the tricks the mind plays, and at my unwillingness even to name my destined refuge to myself until I had obtained sustenance for a few days. Did I fear that I would in some manner betray myself to the priests, and that they would then betray me to the King? I do not know, but I suppose something of that sort must have restrained me.

In one campaign against the Philistines I had passed through a glen not far from the Vale of Elah, and had been struck by the strange formation of the land. In that valley, through which a stream flowed even in summer, there stood a steep rocky hill, an isolated stronghold standing apart from the central range of the mountains of Judah. Near the summit were a number of deep caves, and it seemed to me even then that the Lord had made the place as a sure stronghold. It was named Adullam, and thither, by night marches, I made my way.

Adullam was possessed of more than natural advantages. It lay beyond the land which Saul controlled and policed, and yet it was not within the territory of the Philistines. In short, it was in wild border country, bandit country, for the only inhabitants of that region, save for a few shepherds, were broken and lawless men who acknowledged no lord and who lived by raiding their more peaceful but yet distant neighbours. There I thought I might find a refuge; from these men I might raise my own warrior band.

But first, it was necessary to call to me those whom I knew I could trust. There was danger in making the attempt; there was no future unless I did so. I was for some days in sore perplexity as to how it could be contrived. I dared not go myself, for I knew that my father's house would be watched by Saul's agents. Then, returning to my refuge from a hunting trip, I came upon a shepherd watering his flock at the brook. I watched him from behind a rock. He had two boys with him. I sauntered down the hill and greeted him. He immediately looked anxious. A sheepdog growled. I complimented the man on the watchful dog and on his flock.

"What's that to you?" he said.

"Nothing, friend, but I know sheep."

His eyes were fixed on the short sword which hung from my belt. I drew silver from my pouch and jingled it.

"I am looking," I said, "for a man to carry a message for me. Perhaps your older boy would do so."

The boy scowled. I jingled the silver again.

"I would make it worth while," I said.

The younger boy tugged his father's sleeve, and whispered in his ear. The man looked at me intently.

"I could earn more," he said.

The younger boy shook his head, as if to deny that that had been the purport of whatever he had whispered. I let my hand rest on the hilt of my sword.

"You might," I said. "But then, you might not. It's a long way from here to the King, but it is the first step you would find most dangerous."

"Aye," the shepherd said, "I know you for a man of blood. The boy will go if the price is right."

I tossed him some coins.

"The same again," I said, "when he returns. He is to go to Bethlehem, seek out the house of Jesse, my father, and ask for my brother Shammah. He must then tell Shammah where I am to be found, and that he is to come to me with as many men as he can raise." I looked the boy in the face. "If you deceive me," I said, "may the Lord have mercy on your soul, for your father and your brother's blood will be on your hands." I beckoned to the younger boy. "You come with me. I'll take him as a hostage for his brother's good behaviour. Bring one of your father's lambs."

Would I have acted differently if the boy, Laish, had not been beautiful? Probably not, for it was only prudent to take him as a hostage, but at first glance I had noted his dark eyes, his curving lips and the strong straight legs which his short tunic revealed. I had been alone for seven days now. I missed Michal, and I have always loathed to practise the sin of Onan. That night I took him after we had eaten. He gave himself to me with a lust equal to mine. "I have dreamed of you, my lord David," he said, "since I first heard tell of how you slew Goliath"; and our tongues danced together as we wrestled. "When my brother returns," he said, "I shall stay with you." He giggled. "My brother does it with sheep," he said. "Most shepherd boys do," I murmured, "but I never cared to myself, and . . ." I pushed back the matted hair from his face and kissed him. He laughed again: "I would rather play the ewe than the ram," he said; and turned himself round in my arms, pushing his buttocks against me. Later, I said, "But it will not be long before you prefer the ram's part, Laish. You are only a boy now. When my friends come, I shall make you my armour-bearer."

Three days later, towards evening, Shammah arrived with half a dozen men. I gave Laish's brother what I had promised and dismissed him, with a warning of what would happen to him if he revealed our whereabouts. He looked as sullen as before, and I wondered if I would have been wiser to have despatched him. I do not think Laish would have objected, and I could see that some of my new companions thought I was foolhardy to trust his silence. But I have ever preferred not to shed blood unless it is imperative. The Lord loveth those who are merciful.

Shammah told me he had left messages and instructions for other friends, and that he expected we would soon receive reinforcements. I had trusted that he would do so, for I knew that our position remained dangerous until I had gathered a large enough force to enable me to do more than lurk in the caves – however agreeable in other respects Laish made the sojourn there.

Soon, the promised men began to arrive. The sons of my half-sister Zeruiah – Joab, Abishai, and Asahel – were among the first to join me. I received Joab with mixed feelings. On the one hand, I was never easy with him. Whatever services he did me, I could never overcome the feeling of repulsion he inspired in me. On the other hand, it was testimony to my own reputation that a man so able and ambitious should have abandoned Saul's service for mine. Yet there was something unsettled and unsettling about him. He was now fierce in his denunciation of Saul and his whole family, and even said that he wished he had killed the lot of them before he came to me.

It was characteristic of Joab that he should be quick to tell me that Saul had already given Michal to another man as wife, that he should suggest she had not gone unwillingly, and that he should take a malicious pleasure in being the bearer of such news. Characteristic too that, having done so, he should glance at Laish and say,

"But I see the news is less likely to pain you than I had supposed."

His brothers were of a different temper, Abishai stolid and utterly trustworthy, Asahel light, spirited, handsome, and full of joy.

Our little band grew in numbers and I set Joab to train them. Whatever his faults, I have never denied him military skill; and I knew that he understood what I wanted of my men and would make them ready for my purpose.

One evening, when the cooks were preparing supper, the watchman called to warn of a new arrival. The man climbing the hill was in a state of exhaustion, falling over two or three times and struggling with difficulty to his feet. I sent Laish and Asahel down to help him; and when they brought him to me, the ragged remnant of his garment revealed him to be a priest.

At first he was beyond speech, but when he had been given soup and wine, he revived sufficiently to be more aware of where he was. Seeing me, he fell to the ground at my feet, and, when I had raised him up, he said he was Abiathar, son of Abimelech, priest of Nob, and "the last of the house of Eli". The story which he told, in a voice broken with frequent sobs and much sighing, was terrible.

Saul, he said, had held a council some days after my flight. He sat under a tamarisk tree in Ramah, with a spear in his hand, and cursed his councillors for their failure to apprehend me. He accused them of conspiring against him, and of being in league with Jonathan who had betrayed him and allied himself to me.

"Is there not one man," he cried, "who is loyal and who will help me find my enemy?"

At that moment Doeg the Edomite pushed himself forward and fell on his knees before the King. He told him of my visit to Nob and of how Abimelech had given me provisions.

So Saul sent for Abimelech and the other priests of Nob, and accused them of aiding his enemy. Abimelech protested that, to the best of his knowledge, I was a loyal servant of the King, and that he had believed that in helping me, he was fulfilling the King's wishes. How was he to know that the husband of the King's daughter and slayer of Goliath was become Saul's enemy? His defence drove Saul to still greater fury, all the more, I suppose, because his words were so evidently true, and therefore unanswerable. Crying out that he would not argue with a traitor, Saul commanded his servants to cut him down. Not a man moved, till Doeg the Edomite came forward, and drawing a sword, struck Abimelech in the neck. When he fell to the ground, he cut off his head, and then turned on the other priests who stood too terrified to move. This was the signal for a general massacre. According to Abiathar more than eighty priests were killed; and he himself escaped only by feigning death and then creeping away when night fell.

This story moved us all deeply.

I took Abiathar in my arms and said:

"I am much to blame. I knew when I saw Doeg the Edomite that he would tell Saul of my visit, and though I could not anticipate that Saul would take such terrible revenge for what your father had done in all innocence, nevertheless I have been the cause of the death of all your house. I beg therefore that you remain with me, and I promise you that I shall keep you safe."

Nevertheless, as I lay under the stars, with Laish sleeping beside me, I could not but reflect on the mysterious working of the Lord who ensures that out of evil comes good: for no one now in my service could have any doubt as to what his fate would be if he fell into Saul's hands. Therefore, it seemed to me, the King's violence and cruelty had done me a service, by binding my men firmly to my cause.

The small town of Keilah – an Israelite settlement, about an
hour's march from our caves – was being besieged by a Philistine
force. I resolved that we should relieve it, and make it our base. It
was clear to me that if I was to lead anything more than a troop
of bandits, I must establish my reputation as a leader capable of
succeeding where Saul was failing, and of protecting our fellow
countrymen from the terrors of the Philistines. Nor could I forget
that I was Saul's anointed successor. The King had turned on me
for that reason, rewarding my loyalty with persecution. He had
driven me into the wilderness, but I would make the wilderness
my point of departure rather than my fate.

"We can," I told my officers, "set up a principality of our
own, a frontier state, independent of Saul and secure from the
Philistines."

My determination was not well received. This surprised me.
If my followers were not prepared for such a venture, why, I
asked, had they joined me?

"Was it merely to act as brigands and jackals?"

To his credit Joab, never lacking in intelligence, though
sometimes in judgement, saw the force of my argument; and
where Joab led, others, who recognised his stolidity but feared
my audacity even while admiring it, were ready to follow. It irked
me that Joab and I should be so intimately and necessarily joined;
but I recognised the value of the bond that held us together.

We attacked the Philistine camp at dawn. I have often observed
that besiegers of a town are in a precarious or vulnerable
condition, unless their commander has both the intelligence

and the resources to protect himself against a relieving force. This Philistine commander, whose name I have forgotten, lacked at least the intelligence. His forces were concentrated against the walls of Keilah, and it did not seem to have occurred to him to guard his rear. We scattered his army before the sun was up. There was little resistance and we did not lose a single man. The gates of Keilah were opened to us, and we were received as heroes and liberators. The townsfolk's gratitude survived even the attack my men made on their wine-cellars. I called the elders together and informed them that henceforth they were under my protection; that they were absolved from loyalty to Saul who had abandoned them to the Philistine wolves, and that they should now regard me as their lord. I invited them to give donations to the supply of my soldiers' needs; and they did not refuse.

I valued my little triumph for another reason: it reminded the Philistines that I was a man to be reckoned with. Of course I knew that there was little prospect of my soon being in a position to encounter the main Philistine army on equal terms; but that did not distress me. I saw, though I concealed this even from my officers, that the time could come when I might need to make friendly advances to the Philistines, if Saul's purpose towards me remained unchanged; and it seemed good that by this small independent venture I should have shown myself formidable.

Meanwhile I sent a message to Saul in which I declared that the misery of Israel had compelled my actions, and that I would hold Keilah to protect the frontier. There was perhaps an underlying insolence in this declaration, which was likely to infuriate the King. Again, I judged that the moral effect of my expression of confidence would do me no harm among those in Saul's army who were aware of his declining powers, and who were also dismayed by my banishment and by Jonathan's disgrace.

My satisfaction was short-lived. Keilah was a small place. It was not easy to accommodate my men who, after their sojourn in the wilderness, were not, I confess, the most agreeable of guests for the townspeople, whose initial gratitude was soon replaced by grumbling. Relations between them and my men deteriorated. The mayor of Keilah, who found his own importance diminished by my presence, proved obstructive. To teach him better manners, and to impress the people by my severity, I dismissed him from office and put him under house arrest. Joab was all for having him flogged, the more so when he heard that the mayor had declared that we were vicious and ungodly men, David committing abomination with Laish, and Joab with Elhanan, the son of Dodo of Bethlehem. I sympathised with Joab's anger, but believing that to flog the mayor would anger the townspeople, refused to agree to it. I contented myself with taking the mayor's wife to my bed, and making sure that he knew I had done so.

This incident made me reflect, however. It was natural of course that while we lived as outlaws – six hundred men without women – there should be several of us guilty of what the priests deem to be an offence against the Lord; men, especially soldiers, must have relief, and, if they are deprived of women, will take it where they find it. I did not believe in any case that my connection with Laish was vicious. Nevertheless I did not deceive myself by supposing that the rumour of our relations would not harm my reputation, however natural my men found it. My feelings for the boy were tender and loving as well as lustful; yet, even as I held him in my arms under the night sky, I longed for Michal, for the man who has enjoyed the love of women, can never find true satisfaction in a boy. The act may be delightful, and yet there is a futility to it, for it exists only in and for itself. The mayor's wife was a fat woman, older than myself, unskilled in the art of love, and passive as dead meat in my embraces. Even so, she gave me what my poor and lovely Laish could never give.

Word came that Saul was marching against Keilah; and it was clear that his arrival would be welcomed by the townspeople, whose resentment of our presence and demands was already allowing them to forget how I had delivered them from the hand of the Philistines. Joab was all for holding the little town and defying Saul; but it was doubtful if we could do so unless the men of Keilah stood by us. And I did not believe they would. To persuade Joab of this, I had Abiathar, as a priest, take the auspices so that we might know the word of the Lord. To my question whether the men of Keilah would stand by me or would rather surrender me to Saul, the answer was unequivocal. We therefore prepared to depart, first setting light to the roofs of the houses to teach the ingrates better manners.

We withdrew south of Hebron, beyond the reach of Saul, where we sustained ourselves by levying tribute on the farmers whose lands we in turn protected from marauders.

The chief landowner of the district was a man by the name of Nabal, rich in flocks of both sheep and goats. At the time of the sheep-shearing, we watched over his men by Carmel, and when the shearing was done, I sent a detachment of my men to Nabal. Asahel led the deputation, being the best-spoken and most personable of my officers. I instructed him to speak to Nabal in polite and diplomatic fashion. He was to tell him how we had guarded his shearing and ensured that it passed off untroubled; Nabal would find that he had not lost a single sheep or ounce of wool. The care we had taken of them should therefore be rewarded.

"There should be no need," I warned Asahel, "to utter any threat, but it will do no harm if you let him know how many we are, and remind him what I have achieved, and what manner of man I am."

Nabal however was a fool, and flew into a rage. Who was this David? he cried. A fugitive from his king? No better than a bandit, from what he had heard. Let him learn that he, Nabal, had never paid protection money to any brigands and was not going to begin now.

Asahel returned with this impudent message. Naturally I set my response in motion. I had no choice if I was to retain the respect of my men, and that night we marched towards Nabal's estates.

We had not gone far, however, when my scouts reported a caravan advancing towards us.

Thinking that perhaps Nabal had had second and wiser thoughts, I gave the order to halt, while, prudently, also commanding Joab to prepare the men for battle.

The caravan approached, and a figure detached itself from the band and advanced towards us alone. There was a moon, and the emissary was still some way distant when I saw that it was a woman. I let her come close towards us, far ahead of the caravan, before I moved to greet her. When I did so, she fell to her knees.

Then she lifted her head and spoke, asking first if she was addressing David, the future ruler of Israel. She was Abigail, she said, the wife of Nabal, and she had brought me the gifts which her husband had denied me. She begged me to forgive him his folly, which she would have prevented if she had been present when my men approached him.

"Take what I bring as a peace offering," she said, "that there may be no blood feud between the powerful house of Nabal and my lord David."

I of course had no wish to shed unnecessary blood, and sent my men forward to bring in the asses on which she had loaded her gifts. Finding them satisfactory, I sent her home with the assurance that she had prevented the shedding of blood and, by winning my gratitude and friendship, had preserved her husband from the consequences of his stupidity and ill manners.

Even so, I sent an escort of fifty men with her, to ensure that she did not suffer from Nabal's anger which I was certain her actions would have aroused.

Abigail, dewy-eyed with the excitement of betraying her husband, was apprehensive of his anger. Returning, she found him so drunk as to be beyond understanding. In the morning, as he lay crapulous on the couch, she told him what she had done. He roared his anger, and struck her. She screamed, alerting my men. They thrust the guard at the chamber door aside, and finding Nabal standing over his wife who lay quivering on the floor, silenced the fool. I do not think it was the blow that killed him, for he lingered some days before dying. No doubt it was the Lord's will that he should suffer from his folly. Abigail assured me that he had had an apoplectic fit.

When I learned of Nabal's death, I at once sent for Abigail to make her my wife. She consented without demur, and came to me with some of her waiting-women. It was to one of these, by name Ahinoam, a small smiling girl with black mischievous

eyes, that my first son was born nine months later. I called him
Amnon.

I surrendered Laish to Asahel who had long admired him, and
who also married another of Abigail's women.

The situation of my little army was still perilous. We remained
in the rough country south of Hebron, and lived by necessary
exactions from the farmers there, who however benefited from
the protection from bandits which we provided. Yet, farmers
being by nature ungrateful, our presence was unwelcome; and
indeed there were times when I regretted the burden that we
imposed upon them. Yet things could not have been otherwise.
We were too weak to challenge Saul in open battle, which in
any case I was reluctant to do, on account of the respect I still
felt for him and also because of my enduring love for Jonathan.
Yet it irked me to be compelled to live in this fashion. Time
was slipping by, and I, who had been so briefly and splendidly
one of the Great Ones of Israel, found my ambition stalled, my
genius without satisfying employment. The songs I sang to the
Lord were melancholy in these desert months. Moreover, some
of my men were oppressed by the seeming futility of our way
of life. Joab grumbled at our inaction, and that disturbed me;
his dissatisfaction might prove infectious, and I knew that his
loyalty was never more than provisional.

11

Word was brought that Saul was marching against us, with a great army. Some said it numbered five thousand, others ten. We had no means of knowing which estimate was correct; but it was certain that the King's force greatly outnumbered ours, and that we could not hope to confront it in open battle. In any case I had no wish to embroil Israel in civil war and fraternal struggle. I was, despite Joab's impatience, content to bide my time.

It was approaching the end of summer. The harvest had been brought home, and we extracted sufficient provisions from the reluctant farmers. I knew that Saul would be unlikely to maintain the campaign into the winter, for even if his force was only as large as the lowest estimate, he would have no means of provisioning it in the field when the autumn rains arrived, and the cold weather set in. Besides I had reason to believe that Saul himself was no longer capable of sustaining a long campaign. Those who brought secret word to me, intermittently, from the King's camp, all assured me that Saul was suffering both mental and physical decline. Some said he went drunk every night to bed; if he did so, I pity him, for I believe he drank to banish or subdue the demons which tormented him. Others said that he had fallen into the habit of consulting witches and necromancers, vile wretches who pretend to a knowledge of the future which no man or woman may possess; for the future is known only to the Lord, who guards His secrets from us for His own inscrutable reasons. Or so the priests say; for my part, I believe that the Lord leaves the will of man free and only intervenes to control the larger shape of our destiny. I pondered such matters often in those years in the wilderness, and have found no reason to alter my opinion since. Man's knowledge of himself and his circumstances extends no further than the light of a little candle in a great hall.

My strategy in response to Saul's pursuit was to withdraw before him, to retire into the wilderness of Ziph, and the high hills where my men, now accustomed to rough living, would have the advantage in any skirmish that was forced upon us. But I was confident that we could avoid battle and that Saul's army would soon exhaust itself in vain pursuit of an enemy that seemed as insubstantial as a shadow. My strategy was successful. Often we were within a few miles of Saul, and yet he had no intelligence of our presence. Some of my men were eager for battle, but the greater part relished the game I was playing.

Now it so happened that on a certain night, in the interval between the old moon and the new, Saul was encamped within a half-hour's march of our own refuge, and yet ignorant of how near he was to his intended prey. As I made the round of our outposts, I was seized by a sudden impulse to remind the King of what manner of man I was. So I told Abishai, Joab's brother, the captain of the night watch, and I pointed to the flickering fires of the King's camp in the valley below us. Abishai was a man of no imagination, but absolute fidelity and reliability, as ready to follow and trust me as the sheepdogs I used to train in my boyhood.

So, with only a brief word to our outposts, we descended the hillside in the dark of night, using no light, but trusting to the awareness which our experience of fugitive life had made second nature to us. Saul, over-confident, or simply on account of his failing powers, had posted an inadequate guard, and we slipped through the outer cordon of his camp without difficulty. Over-confidence must have been the reason, I later concluded, for Abner was with the King, and as an experienced and skilled tactician would certainly have ensured that the guard was more tightly drawn, had he not been the victim of faulty intelligence. Yet, even as I write these words, doubt arises; for the truth was that by this time, as I later discovered, Saul's behaviour had grown so erratic that not even Abner dared either to argue with him or surreptitiously correct, as he had been accustomed to do, any blunders which the King might make. Saul had indeed arrived at a sad condition in which his anger was easily aroused against anyone who did not seem to be in utter agreement with him. The truth is that by this stage Saul was no longer fit to be either king or general of the army; but since he was both, Israel suffered.

We knew of course the layout of the King's camp, and so Abishai and I, once within the lines, moved with the confidence and freedom of men going about their proper business; such behaviour is usually unquestioned, and the night was too dark for any to see our faces and so recognise us. It would be an exaggeration to suggest that once within the lines we were out of danger, for mischance is always possible. However, we did what we could to eliminate the risk that any would stop and question us by the certainty with which we made our way towards the King's tent.

That was a perilous moment, for the tent was sure to be guarded by sentries. But a great, a miraculous, stillness hung over all; it was as if the whole of the royal army was caught in a drugged sleep. There were no sentries; we entered the tent unchallenged, and found ourselves standing over the sleeping body of the King as he lay on his pallet, an oil-lamp on a stool beside him, for Saul now experienced all the terrors of darkness, and like a little child feared to be without light in the event of waking before morning.

His spear was thrust in the earth beside him, where his right hand could seize it the moment that he waked. But his slumber was deep. He lay on his back snoring loudly, and the fumes of wine were heavy about him. Abishai laid his hand on the spear.

"David," he whispered, "the Lord has delivered your enemy into your hand."

He pulled the spear from the earth and held it out to me.

"Kill him with his own spear. Then let us slip away, and it will be thought that he has been slain by one of his own men. Nobody suspects that we are here. We can escape as easily as we came in. It will be thought someone weary of his madness and no longer trusting him to lead Israel has put an end to his life. Then either Jonathan who is your friend will be king, and you will be restored to your rightful position, or people will remember Samuel and call on you as the Lord's Anointed."

Perhaps he did not say all this. Perhaps these were only the thoughts that I read in his eyes. Perhaps I attribute to poor, stolid, unimaginative Abishai the thoughts that ran in my own head.

Let me be honest, as I have never been the many times I have recounted the story of this exploit – boring my sons with it, I fear, even my beloved Absalom and certainly that chilly and fastidious Solomon, to whom the idea of creeping down a steep hillside and into the camp of the enemy must seem unthinkable. I have always pretended that I rejected Abishai's suggestion at once. (In telling the story I have given Abishai the words I have written for him here, sometimes indeed making them more forceful and more highly coloured.) I have always presented myself as magnanimous, as one to whom the thought of killing Saul was utterly repugnant.

But of course it was not like that. Stories are rarely the way we like to tell them. I took the spear from Abishai and weighed it in my hand. I wondered, absurdly, whether it was the same spear that Saul himself had hurled at me while I sang in that vain attempt to cure his madness. I put the tip of it to his throat and pricked the skin so that a drop of blood stood out, growing like a ripening cherry. Saul did not stir from his drunken stupor; his snores continued to reverberate, I drew the spear back, and held it high, in both hands, above his heaving belly. There was a moment – I still feel its thrill – when I was about to strike.

What stopped me? What indeed? I wish I could say it was fear of the Lord who has given the commandment: "Thou shalt not kill". I wish I could say that, truthfully. It may have been prudence. In my right mind I knew that Saul was now launched, hell-bent, on a course, a way of life, that must lead to disaster, for all the reality he recognised was now to be found only in his disturbed mind. Subsequently I have thought that I desisted because of my own position as the Lord's Anointed. If Israel's king should fall victim to an assassin, what hope for his successor? But I do not think it was that. I think I spared Saul because at that moment there came into my mind the picture of him advancing towards me when I first cured his madness, when he extended his hand and touched my cheek and I felt his fingers warm and the hand steady, as he said, "I have been away and you have brought me back."

So I said to Abishai, "No."

He looked at me without understanding.

"No," I said again, "I cannot do it."

"Then give me the spear," he said, "and I will make an end of this murderer of priests."

"*No*, Abishai," I said, "extinguish that oil-lamp, and I shall take Saul's spear, and I assure you, though you don't understand me now, we shall have won a greater victory and higher renown than if we had indeed killed Saul."

It was perhaps unkind, knowing, as I did, Saul's terror of the dark, to have put out and then removed his lamp, but I did not see why he should escape scot-free, and in any case he was sleeping so heavily that I thought it unlikely he would wake before it was light.

In the morning as the sun touched the hills with rosy fingers I advanced to a ledge on a spur of the hill overlooking the King's camp. Laish was with me, and he blew loudly on a ram's horn to alert those in the valley below. Then I cupped my hands, and in the clear silence of the mountain air, called out loudly for Abner. There was a delay, and Laish blew on the horn again, a mocking and defiant note, and then I saw Abner advance to the fringes of the camp. I raised my voice, and employing the high rhetorical language which is deemed suitable for formal exchange between great personages, I called out:

"Are you not a valiant man, Abner, and a worthy guardian of King Saul? Go to the King's tent, and seek the spear that stood in the earth by his bed, and the lamp that watched over him by night. Go, seek them, and ask whither they have gone . . ."

Then I drew back, motioning to Laish to do the same, lest any enterprising archer should let an arrow fly, for, though I think we were perhaps out of range of all but the strongest bowman, it is always wise to take precautions. But I was still aware of a great scurry and commotion in the camp below, and I laughed to see men running here and there in panic and uncertainty.

The camp fell silent, and I could see men draw back, as if in shame, and a voice was raised to the hills where we lay concealed, a voice quavering and uncertain, but which I yet recognised as the voice of Saul.

"Is that you, David?" he cried. "Is that you, my son David?"

And I stepped forward into the King's vision, for I felt certain that Saul was filled with shame and that for the moment I was safe to let myself be seen; and I called out in appeal:

"It is I, David, who speaks to Saul, my lord and master, and look, this is the spear in my hand which last night I took from the tent where you slept. Touch your neck, my lord king, and feel the spot where I pricked you when you lay at my mercy. If I had wished to do you evil, nothing but my will and the Lord's mercy prevented me. Does that not prove to you that I am not your enemy? Why then do you hunt me like a wild beast in the hills?"

There was a long silence. Saul sat on a rock and covered his face with his hands as if he was wrestling with the devils that fought to hold him in their power. And the army stood motionless and watching while I was aware of my own men hidden among the rocks above, and felt I could hear them hold their breath as they awaited the King's reply.

At last the King got unsteadily to his feet. He advanced, leaning heavily on Abner till he stood beyond the camp, and within a bowshot of my men.

"Forgive me, David, my son," he cried. "Return to me, and I swear I shall not harm a hair of your head, and that you may fulfil your destiny."

Then he sobbed again and swayed, and would have fallen but for Abner's support.

I believe he was at that moment sincere, and that the love which he had once felt for me had surged up again in his breast – and I wished I could have trusted him. But I knew he spoke only out of the emotion of the moment. So I called out to Abner and told him to send a young man, one of his officers, to me, to retrieve the King's spear "and the oil-lamp", I said, "that guards the King against the terrors of the night while his sentries sleep".

In my mind's eye I see Abner flush with shame, though of course at that distance I could see no such thing. Yet I knew him well enough to understand how he felt, and part of me regretted the humiliation to which I had exposed him.

Abner bent his head, and led the King away, and in a little while an officer emerged from the camp and mounted the hill towards me. I recognised him as Adonijah, a friend of Jonathan, and so, knowing I had nothing to fear, advanced towards him and embraced him. I sent Laish back up the hill to fetch wine, and Adonijah sat beside me on the rock-ledge overlooking the King's camp. I asked after Jonathan and whether he was still in disgrace.

"Saul will never trust him again," was the reply, "because of you, David."

Laish brought the wine, and I sent him away.

"Tell Jonathan," I said, "that I remember the promises we exchanged."

Adonijah said: "I ought to be jealous of you, David. No one can take your place in Jonathan's life. He has lovers, of course, but no one can take your place."

"I was a boy," I said. "Now I am a man. Jonathan understands that."

"Yes," he said, "Jonathan understands too much – and himself too well – for his own happiness or comfort."

I passed Adonijah the goatskin, and watched him as he drank. He was a handsome young man, with sadness in his eyes.

"There was a message for me in what you said. If the King cannot or will not trust Jonathan, then I cannot trust what he said to me just now."

"I would die for Jonathan," he said. "I may have to. The King is like a wind that never blows from the same direction for two days in succession. When he was mad, David, and you cured him, it was different. I was too young to be at the camp then, but I have heard about it, and Jonathan himself has told me of what you did. Of how your music and something else in you drove the demons from his soul. But now they have taken a firm hold of him. They are cunning demons and permit him the appearance of sanity. Sometimes, some days. But deep down, Saul is crazy as a fox. He trusts no one, not even men from his own tribe of Benjamin, not even Abner, who loves him. Saul is in the grip of terrors which he cannot understand and even Abner watches him with horror. Do you know why you managed to get so easily into the King's tent last night? Because his voices had told him to beware of his own guards and so he had dismissed them. The slaughter of the priests of Nob preys on his mind. I have heard him say he is so deep in blood that . . . I forget what. Something terrible, something mad. There are days when he talks only of old Samuel and of the curse the priest laid upon him, and then he says, sometimes, 'Because I am accursed, nothing can now be forbidden me', and then he reverses the sentence and proclaims that on account of the curse, he is capable of nothing. Anything, nothing, it is all the same to him. I tell you, David, if you had killed the King when he lay at your mercy, and if you had then marched openly into the camp and announced what you had done, even Abner would have felt relief that Saul's torment and the fear Saul inspires were at rest."

"I am the Lord's Anointed," I said, "and my promise to Jonathan not to harm his house or family must include Saul."

"Do you understand yourself, David?"

"No, does anyone? Understand himself? Only the Lord can read our hearts."

Adonijah shook his head. He drank some more wine and passed the goatskin back to me, and stretched out his legs in the sun.

"Do you know what Jonathan says about you? That all men desire you, and all women too. He says that even if Saul did not believe the story that Samuel had anointed you as the Chosen of the Lord, which he has known for certain since Samuel's will was discovered after the murder of the priests of Nob, he would still feel about you as he does, that his feelings for you are a compound of love, jealousy, fear, and hatred. But Jonathan says, it is Saul himself Saul fears and hates. It was a bad day for Saul when he came to Samuel in search of those lost asses belonging to his father Kish. I have never lain with a woman," he said, "you must find that strange."

"Strange, yes."

"And reprehensible?"

"There is a boy in my troop, the boy who brought us wine, who feels as you do, and he is one of the bravest fighters among my men. We are what we are, Adonijah. Jonathan is a good man. I am the Chosen of the Lord – oh yes, the story about old Samuel and the anointing is true – so if Samuel spoke the words of the Lord, then I am indeed His Chosen One; and yet I am not a good man as Jonathan is. Do you understand what I am saying? The nature of man is mysterious, intricate, twisted like an old olive tree. Only a rare few, like Jonathan, grow straight as a pine."

"He has a lame son," Adonijah said, "a cripple, called Mephibosheth. He is so gentle with him. The little boy is not quite as others, his wits wander, but Jonathan is so gentle and loving with him. I wish you could see it, the way he cares for him, the way he holds him in his arms. I wish I could join you, David, and share your fortunes, but I cannot leave Jonathan, though I fear that Saul will lead us to disaster."

"Jonathan," I said, "is fortunate to have you. And now you must return to the army, or Saul will think we are conspiring against him. Assure Jonathan that I love him as I have always done and that my heart goes out to him in his perplexities."

Then he rose and we embraced, and his long eyelashes were damp with tears.

"Wait," I said, "you have forgotten Saul's spear and lamp."

He took them up, and said,

"Saul would be better, and we might all be safer, if I left the spear with you."

"Nevertheless," I said, and watched him descend the hill to the army and the King he feared.

I never saw him again. He fell by Jonathan's side in the doomed battle of Mount Gilboa of which I shall write more fully later. But that conversation has stayed with me, and the memory of a good and unhappy young man, after whom I chose to name one of my sons.

It is morning. Abishag stretches her young and awakening loveliness and yawns. Oh to be young again, I think, as I selfishly call her over to kiss me. Oh to be dead, I think, as I watch her naked beauty on its way to bathe.

12

The next period of my life is one of which I have always preferred not to speak. Yet the truth is that there was nothing to feel ashamed of in my course, for it was compelled upon me by necessity. There are nations, I understand, which recognise Necessity as a goddess, and though, by reason of my upbringing, and experience, I acknowledge no god but the Lord God of Hosts, the God of Israel, who has led me through the dark vale of fear and terrible danger to the sunny uplands – may His name be blessed – yet I confess there have been moments when I have felt the temptation to envy those peoples who have a plethora of gods and goddesses, each guarding over a particular activity or part of life. I pray that the Lord of Hosts keeps me from yielding to such temptation, but I admit that, were I to do so, Necessity would be a goddess I would readily acknowledge.

Fortunately there is no need to do so. If Necessity be not a goddess, Necessity is nevertheless a thing, a fact, as hard and harsh and painful as the rock against which you may stub your toe in the dark of night. No one, I have often said, is fit to command an army who does not recognise Necessity, just as the first and rarest quality a general requires is the courage and wisdom to know when to retreat.

That was now my position. My conversation with that unhappy young man Adonijah had convinced me that Saul's repentance of his zeal in pursuing me even unto death would not last long. The turbulence of his spirit would soon drive him once more against me, for I sensed that deep in his tormented mind lurked the suspicion that if he slew me, he would prove, even to his own satisfaction, that Samuel had not spoken the word of the Lord; if I, whom Samuel had anointed with oil as Saul's successor, could be removed from the scene, then it must have appeared to Saul, in his mad perplexity, that Samuel's rejection of him was no more the expression of the Lord's will than Samuel's anointing of me had been. Therefore I could not persuade myself that Saul would not soon renew his pursuit, and, as the weeks passed, and the difficulty of maintaining my little force in the inhospitable mountains of Judah increased, I feared that Saul's next foray might end less happily for me.

Necessity compelled me to shift our quarters, and it seemed to me that I had no choice but to offer my services to the Philistines. I had met Achish, King of Gath, during certain negotiations while I was still in favour with Saul, and he had impressed me as an honest man, though limited, as I said to Joab, Abishai, and Asahel, whom I had called to me to consult concerning our predicament; a man with whom I could do business. Joab was doubtful and raised objections, as I had expected. Abishai was silent; matters of high policy were always beyond him; and I had included him in the conference only because he would have been offended if I had not invited him, and because in the end I knew that his trust in me would lead him to conclude that I was right. The quick-witted Asahel immediately saw the force of my argument. The speed of his understanding was his great virtue, though allied to an imaginative ardour which at times led him to acts of reckless impetuosity. Joab however dug his heels in, and declined to be persuaded.

"I have always said," he said, "that the only good Philistine is a dead one."

I stifled the boredom which this characteristic intonation of a worn-out platitude inspired in me. Joab has ever been full of these cant sentiments. I suppose it is easier to repeat such stuff than to think for oneself.

"Joab," I said, "you know how highly I value your opinion, and especially how I rely on you in matters of strategy and tactics. The quality of our fighting force is entirely the result of your skill as a trainer of men. I know how hard and for what long hours you have worked, and I know that my position would indeed be desperate but for your efforts. It is entirely understandable that, occupied as you have been, you have not had the time which your diligence has granted me to consider the wider aspect of our affairs. But the truth is that we are caught here between the forces of Saul and the forces of Philistia, and of necessity, as winter draws on, our days here are numbered. The time will soon be upon us when we cannot supply the basic needs of our men. Some will then drift away, and your work will have been wasted.

"I have no more love for the Philistines than you. Believe me, there is scarce one that I would trust, and if I make an exception of Achish of Gath, it is only because I have seen enough to be persuaded that he is not your typical Philistine, but a man of honour and decency. Even so, I would not dare to approach him but for one thing: and that is your achievement in forming our men into such a formidable army. We have something to offer him which no king will decline and at the same time a force sufficiently well-trained and disciplined to deter him from treachery, even if my assessment of his character is mistaken. But our choice, my dear Joab, is straightforward: we must entrust ourselves and the safety of our wives, children, and loved ones, either to Achish or to Saul. You know Saul too well to believe that any man, let alone those who have offended him as pre-eminently you and I have done, can rely on him in his disturbed and tormented condition; therefore, reluctantly, I have to urge you to agree with me that, of the two evils, an approach to Achish is the less dangerous."

Naturally my flattery had its effect; Joab, who has always believed himself to be less highly valued than is his due, was for the moment appeased. Of course he continued for some time to grumble and protest, but he did so only as a matter of form, to emphasise the strength of his will and the independence of his mind, both of which my words had however subverted.

Negotiations with Achish were as easy and agreeable as I had expected. He was intelligent enough to realise that the adherence of my well-trained little army would greatly strengthen his own position in the rivalry that was endemic among the kings of

Philistia, the divisions among whom were, under the Lord, the salvation of the Children of Israel. The strength and continued military superiority of the Philistines were sufficient – despite the reforms I had initiated in Saul's army – to destroy the Children of Israel utterly and subjugate our people, especially now that Saul was not what he had formerly been; only the inability of the Philistines to maintain unity and harmony among themselves prevented this – testimony, as I have always known, to the superiority of the Lord God of Israel over the idols that the Philistines worship; for, as I have written, "except the Lord guard the city, the watchman waketh but in vain". In more prosaic moments, however, I have recognised that the discord among our enemies, even those of the same race, is a great aid to the protection in which the Lord of Hosts enfolds us.

My confidence was justified. It rested, I am bound to confess, not only in my certainty that Achish's intelligence would be sufficient to let him realise the value of the strength I brought him, but also in my awareness of the admiration which he had developed for me at our previous encounter.

It was therefore with real warmth that he embraced me and with sincerity that he declared himself delighted that I should have joined myself to him. Moreover, he added that nothing could gratify him more than the trust I laid upon him.

"We have fought hard against each other, David, and learned in battle to acknowledge each other's virtue. May we who were the best of enemies henceforth and for ever be the best of friends."

Naturally I assented to this proposal and told him that his generosity filled my heart with gladness.

He gave a great feast of welcome and himself became sentimentally and agreeably drunk; Joab was sullen and sodden drunk, but, even in that condition, ever watchful and suspicious. I drank moderately, as has always been my way, but did not remain so offensively sober as to let my superiority to the company be too apparent. Moreover, like Joab, though perhaps for more subtle reasons, I remained watchful. I knew that there were many chiefs among the Philistines who had reason to resent me, for I had deprived them of sons, brothers, or fathers, and on some occasions, carried their daughters away. I knew also that there were those among them who were jealous of Achish and who would not be slow to take any opportunity to remove him. For, to this extent, Joab's hostility to the Philistines was justified. They are by nature treacherous, for there is none among their gods and goddesses who requires of them the truth, as the Lord God of Israel does; and for this reason, they think it no shame to break their word, and do not understand the concept of loyalty. Achish was a rare exception among them, and I believe his mother was an Israelite captive from my own tribe of Judah, made slave and concubine to the King's father.

It was not long before I became aware of murmurings against us. To this extent I had miscalculated, not making full allowance for the mean and selfish temper of the Philistines. I had thought that more than Achish would recognise the value of my presence at the head of an army of six hundred men; but any such recognition was prevented by resentment, and I soon realised that not only were we in some danger, but that Achish's friendship for me threatened his own position. Philistines think nothing of murdering a king; indeed it is a common practice among them, however abhorrent and vile we Israelites think it.

I therefore approached Achish and suggested that it might be to our common advantage if he would grant me an independent post, preferably on the frontier with the Amalekites (enemies of both Israel and Philistia) where I could serve him in a manner less likely to enflame his nobility and captains.

Achish, being as I have said as intelligent as he was virtuous, immediately responded to the force of my argument. He assigned me to the command of the little town of Ziklag, half a day's march from Gath, and perpetually threatened by the Amalekites and the other hostile tribes that inhabited the southern borderland. I made it my business to protect the inhabitants of Ziklag by launching punitive raids against the enemies who had tormented them for so many years. These raids served the double purpose of maintaining the fighting quality of my little army and endearing me to the citizens of Ziklag, whom I not only relieved from fear but enriched by the spoils of war. They soon became devotedly attached to me, to such an extent indeed that when I finally established myself as king, first of Judah and then of all Israel, they continued to accept me as their lord.

Since I never intended that my sojourn among the Philistines should be enduring, and was ever mindful that I was the Lord's Anointed, I naturally endeavoured to confine my raids to the territory of those tribes which had long been enemies of the Israelites as well as of the Philistines. If I occasionally let it be understood that I also launched attacks against the cities of Judah, this was merely because I deemed it necessary to do so to persuade Achish of my wholehearted loyalty, and that I had altogether cut the bonds that tied me to my own people.

A new crisis soon arose. Saul, enjoying rare moments of lucidity, had recently achieved some success in the frontier skirmishes with the Philistines, while Jonathan had made a daring and successful raid against some of their northern cities. This aroused the Philistines, and persuaded them temporarily to set aside the quarrels between their petty kingdoms and unite themselves in a great army pledged, as they put it, "to exterminate the viper Saul and all his brood".

Naturally Achish summoned me, as his vassal, to join the Philistine host, feeling no hesitation in doing so because he believed that my reported raids into Judah had utterly separated me from my own people. Some of my men, among them the noble Asahel, were dismayed at the prospect of fighting against fellow Israelites alongside our traditional enemies. Joab however thumped the table and said:

"It's the chance we have been waiting for. Wipe out Saul and Samuel's promise will be fulfilled. Blessed," he added perfunctorily, "be the name of the Lord."

I understood Joab. When he deserted Saul to follow me, he had been disappointed at the slow growth of our army; he had thought that David and Joab would attract more defectors, and he had not imagined that our sojourn in the wilderness would be so prolonged and perilous. He had resisted my proposal that we should ally ourselves to Achish, partly because he disliked and distrusted the Philistines, and partly, simply, because it was a new idea; and Joab always required time to adapt to new ideas. Now, though he had not overcome his repugnance for the Philistines, he had reconciled himself to our position. His hatred of Saul and all his family – even including my beloved Jonathan – was so intense that I believe he would have welcomed an alliance with Satan if that would secure the destruction of Saul. He now saw that longed-for moment approach; and in his enthusiasm, he did not perceive the difficulties that were apparent to me. Of course Saul's defeat and, perhaps, his death in battle, would leave the throne of Israel vacant. Yet I could not be confident that all the tribes would welcome me as Saul's successor, even though I proclaimed to them that Samuel had anointed me with oil as the Chosen of the Lord, if I had fought in the Philistine army against Saul and Israel. It was possible that Achish would establish me as a puppet king in Israel, and that, once king, I might gradually be able to free myself from Philistine bonds; but even that did not appear to me to be a happy solution; it was not how I wished to become King of Israel.

I prayed long to the Lord that He would guide my footsteps on the path of righteousness and so enable me to fulfil the promise I had made Him through the mediation of Samuel. I allayed the fears and uncertainties of my men by telling them to put their trust in the Lord of Hosts, whose mind no man could know, but whose purpose was fixed and who guided our goings-out and our comings-in. I reminded them of the travail of our forefathers as they wandered forty years in the wilderness after their deliverance from Egypt. I also remarked to Achish that, though as his vassal and fully aware of the debt of gratitude I owed him, I would naturally, willingly and zealously, perform any task he set me, nevertheless I was not so certain that all his countrymen would be happy to see me marching with them against my own people. Achish, I said, had no cause to doubt my loyalty to himself; but others might feel differently.

"I mention this, my dear Achish," I said, "only as a warning to yourself. I should not wish my presence in your army to do anything to disturb your relations with the other kings of Philistia, or even to persuade them to repose less than full confidence in you."

"David," he replied, embracing me, "as ever you speak like a man of honour. But my trust in you is absolute, and I shall assure my fellow commanders it is well founded."

Naturally I professed myself delighted by the confidence in me which Achish displayed; yet I hoped that I might possibly have instilled a little doubt in his noble mind.

Things turned out as I had warned him. When the other Philistine kings heard that I was marching with them, and that Achish even intended to give me command of the right wing of the army, they exploded in anger. David, they said, has deceived Achish; David has bewitched Achish; David has seduced Achish; David is the enemy of Philistia; the quarrel between Saul and David was mere pretence; David is still working for Saul who has sent him among the ranks of the Philistines in order to betray them when the battle is at its fiercest; David, some said, should be put to death as a spy; even if Achish will not assent to that, they said, we all refuse to march as long as David and his men are in the army.

Achish reported all this to me. He was both angry and ashamed.

"I could not imagine," he said, "that even the King of Askelon, who is as loathsome as he is stupid, could sink so low as to accuse me of the abominations he has laid upon me. I shall never forgive him, though he is a cousin of mine, and one day will have my revenge, but now, David, to my utter shame, I must ask you to withdraw yourself and your men from the army, and to retire to Ziklag, where you have made such a success of guarding our southern frontier as would persuade, I should have thought, anyone with half an eye of your virtue and loyalty. Forgive me, David, for this request, and rest assured that it betrays no doubt in my mind as to your absolute loyalty to me and innate virtue."

It was a noble speech and I had little difficulty in responding in suitable manner. I blinked my eyes rapidly several times so that the tears started, though I imagine that Achish supposed that I was attempting to restrain them.

I embraced him, and thanked him in a trembling voice for the trust in me which he had expressed; and I assured him that I would remember his nobility to the day of my death. As indeed I have done.

Moreover, I succeeded in restraining a smile till I had quit his company.

13

I was therefore absent from the last act of the tragedy of Saul; and what I know of it, I know only by that mixture of rumour, hearsay, and speculation, which composes what men call history, or sometimes legend.

Saul in these last days was visited, it seems, by a new and stranger perturbation of his spirit. He no longer suffered that annihilation of the mind which enclosed him within a cloud of night; it was rather as if he moved, heavily and unsteadily, through a damp and clinging mist, seeing nothing, hearing nothing, understanding nothing, and yet still in motion.

In this strange mood he betook himself, as word came of how the Philistines were mustered against him, to consult a woman said to possess the power, by necromantic art, of summoning the dead to reveal themselves to the living and speak with them. In his bright noontime Saul had issued laws banning from the kingdom those who claimed knowledge of the black arts. He had called them liars and charlatans that led men into mischief by their pretended wiles and knowledge of what it is forbidden to know. His attempt was vain as such efforts must always be. The desire of certain men to penetrate, or to believe they have penetrated, beyond the realities of rock and pasture, ploughed land, wind, rain and the changing seasons, can never be rooted out. In the best of men this desire takes the form of communion with the Almighty in desert places; in others, incapable of the humbling of the soul which the Lord demands, it expresses itself in a manner that promises more immediate certainties, delusions and cheats though these must prove to be. Only the cultivation of virtue, by communion with the Almighty, can save the seeker after knowledge from the shades of deception. And yet even as I write this, I know it is not the whole truth, which is rather, as I have learned, tasting the water of bitterness; that it is with man as with the tree: the more he seeks to rise into the clear light of knowledge, the more he must also thrust his roots deep into the earth, down into the dark, the deep, into evil. The fool has said in his heart, "There is no god"; but he who seeks to know God must first learn of what evil he is himself capable, what horrors lurk within him.

So, poor Saul, wretched rag of a man and king, starved himself a day and a night, and ventured to Endor to consult this woman who boasted her ability to call up the spirits of the dead for interrogation; and he did so, I imagine, in a state of self-contempt and loathing.

She penetrated his disguise easily.

"Is it not the King who begs me to call up the spirit of Samuel?" she asked. "And is this not the same King who proclaimed the wickedness of such arts as mine, and would have had me stoned to death or driven from Israel?"

And Saul lay on the ground before her, and licked the dust.

Then she laughed, to see him so abject, and consented to do as he bid, for nothing inspires these necromancers so greatly as the acknowledgment of their power by those who in their right mind would deny it.

By what means she conjured up the semblance of the dead High Priest, I do not know. But certainly those who accompanied Saul averred later that the figure of Samuel rose before him in a cloud of red mist.

Saul, still stretched on the bare earth of the hovel, poured forth the despair that tore at his soul. He cried out that the Lord had abandoned him in his trouble and that he was the most miserable of men. The Philistines had brought a great army against him, and when he sought guidance from the Lord, he heard only the wind in the wilderness. Therefore he had come to Samuel to beg him to intercede with the Lord on his behalf, for only thus could Israel be saved.

I have condensed what was reported to me as incoherent

babble, but I believe this was the essence of Saul's sad and painful prayer.

I do not know either by what means the woman of Endor made the shape she had conjured up in reply to Saul; I suppose that like so many of her vile kind she had the ability to throw her voice so that the words she spoke seemed to come not from her but from another place and from the lips of another being or the semblance of a being.

The words she gave to Samuel were harsh. In this at least she was honest, for she answered as I am certain that Samuel himself, that dour, bitter man, with a long, unforgiving memory, would have spoken. Saul – the message came – had been cast aside by the Lord on account of his disobedience to the word of the Lord whose will he had defied by sparing the Amalekites; therefore the Lord had rejected Saul and all his house, and when Saul went forth into battle, he must go without hope; for so it had been spoken. Saul was doomed, and would perish in the mountains of Gilboa.

Then the vision slipped away and the King wept. The woman gave him bread and wine and the flesh of a fatted calf; I would like to think that she did so out of pity for Saul, but it is more probable that she wished to prolong her triumph and savour the sight of the great King reduced to the state of a helpless and babbling child. At any rate, Saul ate and drank, and took his leave, thanking the woman in a manner that bore traces of his former majesty; but his countenance, men say, was blank as the rock-face that rises sheer from the desert sands; and it was in that spirit that he went forth to his last battle.

When word of his defeat and of the slaughter of Jonathan and his other sons was brought to me in Ziklag, I felt his agony and my heart was sore. Saul himself had fallen on his own sword to avoid being made first captive by the Philistines, and then a thing of mockery to them. The news was brought by a young man who came hotfoot from the battlefield, and he carried with him the crown and bracelet of Saul. He told me what I later discovered was not true: that he had himself slain the wounded Saul at the King's own request. He smiled as he knelt before me, hailing me as king, and smiled again as if he looked for a rich reward. I gazed on him with horror.

"You boast," I said, "of having killed the Lord's Anointed. Look well on the light of day, young man, for you shall never see it again."

Then I gave orders that he be taken from my presence and his eyes put out, for, I said, "Let darkness be his who has consigned Saul to eternal night. But let him live," I said, "that he may come to know the pain of humiliation, and let him beg his bread from those who will know him to be vile. In this way, he who boasts of cruelty will feel the pain of receiving mercy; and while he lives he will be a perpetual reminder to all men that the Lord is just."

He screamed horribly as the deed was performed. When I heard his cries, I shuddered, and then I countermanded my first order, and decreed that he should be kept near me. In this way, I said to myself, I shall have about me an example and a warning of the depths to which men can sink. He remained in my household for seven years, suffering the contempt of all; and then I handed him over to the priests with the instruction that he be given a cell and fed on bread and water, and the opportunity to make his peace with the Almighty. He may still be living there. I do not know.

That night in my chamber, I remembered Saul as he had been in his glorious strength; I remembered with a sharper pain the love Jonathan had for me, and I made a poem:

The beauty of Israel is slain upon Thy high places!
How are the mighty fallen!
Tell it not in Gath, publish it not in the streets of Askelon,
Lest the daughters of the Philistines rejoice,
Lest the daughters of the uncircumcised triumph.

Ye mountains of Gilboa, let there be no dew,
Neither let there be rain, upon you,
Nor fields of offerings;
For there the shield of the mighty is vilely cast away,
The shield of Saul,
As though he had not been anointed with oil.

From the blood of the slain, from the fat of the mighty,
The bow of Jonathan turned not back,
And the sword of Saul returned not empty.

Saul and Jonathan were lovely and pleasant in their lives,
And in their death they were not divided;
They were swifter than eagles,
They were stronger than lions.

Ye daughters of Israel, weep over Saul,
Who clothed you in scarlet, with other delights,
Who put on ornaments of gold upon your apparel.

How are the mighty fallen in the midst of the battle!
O Jonathan, thou wast slain in thy high places.

I am distressed for thee, my brother Jonathan;
Very pleasant hast thou been unto me;
Thy love to me was wonderful, passing the love of women.

How are the mighty fallen and the weapons of war perished!

When I had made this song, I felt a great weariness come
upon me, but my grief was assuaged, for I knew I had done
them honour and my words had given them such immortality
as it was in my power to bestow. Then, since my mind was
filled with the memory of the love which Jonathan had felt for
me, and I for him, and since I did not wish for the company of
women, but feared the thought of solitude, I sent for Laish.

I sang my lament to him, and he broke into weeping.

When he had recovered himself, he said, "But David, Saul
sought you out to kill you, and now you sing so beautifully of
his glory."

"Yes," I said, "do you think I am a hypocrite, Laish?"

"If I thought that I would not have wept."

"But you don't understand?"

He shook his head.

"I don't understand myself," I replied. "I made the song I had
to make. That's all I know. Sometimes, Laish, I think we are
each of us two people, as Saul was. The split, the division of
his nature, was clear and unmistakable in him. But it is there

in all of us. Even as I ordered that wretch to be blinded, I was calculating what advantage I could draw from the death of Saul and Jonathan and from the disaster which has fallen on Israel. I was considering what effect this would have on my relationship with Achish. And yet when I retired to my chamber, I knew only grief, and I made what I have made. I loved Saul once. Then I feared him. Then I pitied him. But I never allowed myself the ignominy of hating him, as he hated me. Yet I believe he struggled against that hatred too. Laish, the nature of man is intricate. For my own sake I had to make this song, to preserve myself from corruption by honouring Saul."

"And Jonathan," Laish said.

"Jonathan," I said, and took him in my arms.

Book II $\int$

Book III

14

Even Asahel was amazed and angry that I did not now declare myself the anointed King of Israel. He was not satisfied with my explanation that I had learned one thing about statecraft: never to take a decision till it was essential and the moment ripe. He shook his head in disbelief when I said I would wait until I was called.

Joab, he said, was furious. Joab could not understand me either. Asahel hesitated, then, in a rush of words, said that his elder brother even wondered if I had lost my nerve.

"Time and patience," I said, "time and patience."

I had sent instead discreet congratulations to Achish on his victory. Then, secretly, and without announcing my intention to him, I removed to Hebron, the chief city of Judah. You must remember that at this time the kingdom of Israel was all but cut in half on account of the continued occupation of Jerusalem by the Jebusites. So now I established myself in Hebron and was accepted as king by the men of Judah, but Abner, who was ever-loyal to the house of Saul, being a cousin to the dead King, though friendly to me, nevertheless established Saul's last surviving son, Ishbosheth, as king in Saul's place. He did so, though he knew Ishbosheth to be a poor creature, dull-witted and sluggish, no soldier but a coward whom Saul had, for his own pride's sake, kept from the army. Abner in his obstinate (but praiseworthy) devotion to Saul's memory made Ishbosheth king, and I honoured him for his loyalty. Joab, jealous of Abner's nobility and renown, argued that Abner intended in time to discard Ishbosheth and make himself king.

"Well," I said, "you know how I trust your judgement, cousin, but we must wait and see. Trust in the will of the Lord. Abner is also of the house of Saul whom the Lord deprived of the kingdom, through the mouth of Samuel, as it was promised to me. But I shall not seek it through blood. To do so would be a grave sin. I have no desire to shed the blood of our fellow Israelites. As I said to your brother, time and patience will resolve matters in our favour."

So I sent a friendly message to Abner and to Ishbosheth, and suggested that we should collaborate against the Philistines. I said nothing of the matter of the kingship, but spoke only as if we were all three equals.

Abner replied in like manner, and proposed a time and place for a conference. The place suggested was Bibeon, which, being some five miles east of Gibeah and six miles north-west of Jerusalem, lay within the territory which Ishbosheth controlled, however ineffectively.

I assented, and then made one of the greatest mistakes of my life. Recognising the danger of going myself, even with a guard and even though I trusted Abner, into such a place, I asked Joab to lead our delegation.

"Ishbosheth himself will not be there," I said, "but their delegation will be headed by Abner, the second man in their kingdom. It is therefore not fitting that I go. It is more proper that you as the second man in Judah should talk with Abner, which you will do as equals. For you, Joab, are of course to me as Abner is to Ishbosheth."

I said this to please Joab by demonstrating my trust in him and my high regard for his abilities; and I chose not to reveal to him that I feared a trap. I did not suspect Abner, but remembering Jonathan's contempt for his brother Ishbosheth, and remembering also how Michal had talked scornfully of him, I was afraid that he might, without Abner's knowledge, have taken this chance to arrange my murder; and so remove the Lord's Anointed, and thus show his people that the curse which Samuel had laid on the house of Saul was a vain thing.

I have reason, which I learned later from Abner himself, to believe that my suspicions were justified, and that there was such a trap laid for me, though Abner was innocent and ignorant of it then. And yet I reproach myself for not having taken the risk, and for having allowed prudence to govern me.

I do so on account of what befell.

The conference began amicably, it was reported, with Abner and Joab recalling past battles against the Philistines, battles in which both men had won glory. Then Abner (apparently) suggested that some of the young men on each side should amuse their elders by taking part in mimic warfare; and Joab agreed, remarking – I am told – that they would doubtless see that the young had much to learn.

It was Laish who, in tears, gave me the most reliable account of what then ensued, he being one of the youths told by Joab to strip for this war game.

"We were wrestling," he said, "and then all of a sudden I saw that one of Abner's young men had drawn a dagger and was making ready to stab his opponent who was Elhanan. I cried out a warning, but too late. The knife slipped between Elhanan's ribs, and he gave a loud cry, and his body slackened in the other's grip. It was horrible, David. One moment, play, and the next, a shambles. For of course when he saw this happen, Joab shouted that we were betrayed, and drew his own sword and all those who had been talking and drinking wine as old companions were at each other's throats. I cannot blame Joab, for we know he loved Elhanan, and yet I believe that if he had acted differently, Abner himself would have despatched the murderer . . ."

As he spoke I remembered that night in the desert, when Azreel slew Nehemiah, Jonathan's sergeant, in a quarrel, and I, acting as both judge and executioner, averted a blood feud by . . .

"Go on," I said to Laish, "but be brief."

"It cannot have been intended," the boy said, "for neither Abner nor any of his men were prepared for battle, while Joab had warned us all in advance to keep a close eye on our weapons, in case we were threatened by a treacherous plot. So we soon put them to flight, even Abner, who had time only to snatch up a spear as he headed for the hills. And Asahel ran after him . . . and did not return . . . It was dusk when we found his body, with a single spear-wound.

"Then we spied Abner and his men as the moon rose, secure from our pursuit on a high hill. And Abner called down to Joab,

"'Shall the sword devour for ever? And Israelite slay Israelite?'"

Laish wept.

"I loved Asahel," he said in a low and broken voice, "and he has been gathered from me. We buried him in the family tomb at Bethlehem, and here we are, David. Abner may have had no choice, but Joab will never forgive him."

To me, Joab said only,

"Now I too must learn to practise patience."

I preached patience, I practised patience, I recognised the need for patience; and nevertheless I wearied of that virtue. "How long, O Lord," I prayed, "how long before Thy servant enter into the kingdom promised him?"

I practised diplomacy also. That can be an enthralling craft. Nevertheless, to describe it is wearisome; to listen to an account of diplomatic manoeuvring intolerable. Though, in Hebron, I strove to govern well, to be both loved and – which is more important – respected by my subjects, I was conscious that the years were passing, and that I was growing older without the chance of fulfilling myself. Joab's impatience irked me. Since Abner's killing of Asahel, Joab was ever more morose and less to be trusted. I feared the onset of a dark spirit which would envelop him and destroy him as the black and evil spirit had crushed poor Saul.

I had few comforts. Occasional letters from the wise Achitophel, Saul's councillor and now his son's, secretly conveyed, assured me that the wretched Ishbosheth's rule grew ever less acceptable to the Children of Israel; and yet Abner remained obstinately loyal and there was no sign of revolt. Achitophel too counselled patience.

To alleviate my boredom, which I feared might lead me to a rash act, I took to myself several wives in Hebron. Now, in old age, beyond love-making, it pains me to try to remember them; and indeed the names of several have quite escaped my failing memory. There was one however who brought me especial delight, and whose image still recurs to me in dreams. Why this should be so puzzles me, for out of that marriage came the most intense mingling of love, fear, hatred, pain and self-reproach; and anger.

Her name was Maacah. She was the daughter of Talmai, King of Geshur, a wretched principality to the north-west of the Sea of Galilee. She was a tawny Arab girl, with eyes the shape and colour of dark olives, and limbs that could outstrip the roe deer in racing. Her temper was fierce as an untamed hound; and she bore me two children: Absalom, my most beloved of sons, and Tamar, the most beautiful of my daughters.

And I shall have more – too much for comfort – to relate of them; if the Lord wills that I should be compelled to do so.

Then, finally, the dissension in the northern kingdom which I had long expected broke out. Ishbosheth, to compound his folly, quarrelled with Abner, ostensibly because Abner had taken possession of a girl who had once been Saul's concubine, and whom he himself desired. The real cause lay deeper. Despite his incapacity Ishbosheth was flattered by his title of king, and had come to believe in the reality of his kingship. Accordingly he more and more resented the dominance which Abner exerted, naturally, both by force of character and by reason of his experience. Abner himself resented the rebuke, publicly delivered to him; his contempt for the King, whom he had elevated only on account of his own devotion to Saul's memory, was intensified. He remembered the affection and respect which he had always felt for me; and so at last he sent ambassadors to suggest that the two kingdoms be reunited, that he himself should dispose of Ishbosheth, and that I should be acknowledged as the rightful King of All-Israel.

For a moment nevertheless I hesitated. I admired Abner and yet could not but suspect that he was luring me into a trap. I therefore set a test for him. I told him I would consent to a meeting only if he at the same time brought Michal, of whom the wrath and jealousy of Saul had deprived me, back to me, restoring her to her rightful position as my wife.

Of course I was deceiving myself. It was not really that I feared a trap. It was rather that I wished this to be the first statement of the new power I was to assume: to demand the restoration of Michal as my condition for meeting Abner. My loss of her – and Saul's immediate disposal of her in marriage – had been the sharpest insult I had ever received. Michal, apart from her other perfections, had been to me the proof of my great success and acceptance as one of the mighty men of Israel. The humiliation of losing her had rankled with me all my years in the wilderness. I had spoken of it to no one. It was as if in losing Michal I had lost part of my manhood; as if, in raping her from me, Saul had made me a eunuch. I knew he had known that, and had rejoiced in his achievement. And so it was necessary that she be restored to me if I was to be made whole again, and as if only thus could the kingdom of Israel be restored itself to full health and fertility.

And yet I awaited her arrival with trepidation and keen anxiety. All my life I have found it easy to dominate women. It is not only because I am king that even now I find no difficulty in coaxing a smile from my little Shunnamite girl; I have never doubted my ability to charm, and the manner of her smile proves to me that that ability has not departed. It is of course natural for men to dominate their womenfolk, and most do; but few – perhaps none – can have found it as easy as David the King. Even Maacah, that wild Arab gazelle of the desert, would flush at my smile and tremble like a tender filly at my touch. That is as it should be.

But Michal from our first meeting insisted on our equality as man and woman, and her smile suggested that she thought her acceptance of that equality a mere pretence. Her pride as the King's daughter was something I never subdued; and even in my fiercest moments, I knew a certain pleasure in myself that I had failed to do so.

Michal herself must have suffered. I could not doubt that, even though I had always doubted that her love for me was equal to mine for her. She had been treated as an object by her father, an object which offered him a means of expressing his resentment against me, in which sentiment, then dominating his disordered heart, he took no thought of his daughter's feelings. He disregarded her pride, which was chief among her emotions, warring only against her self-love and admiration for her own beauty. Careless of what she felt, he had given her in marriage to another, a man unknown to her, and of lowly birth. He had treated his daughter as a man might treat a slave-girl of whom he had tired, disposing her wherever seemed convenient. I could not doubt that Michal had resented this bitterly. I could not doubt either that she had concealed her resentment, for to offer public display of resentment is an offence against one's pride.

But I could not be certain that she would not equally resent what she might presume to understand as a revelation of a feeling in me that was not love for her, but desire simply for possession. In other words – and my words grow ever more confused, like my thoughts, in the waste nights of old age – I feared that she might see me as she saw Saul: the man of power who takes where he pleases and disposes as he pleases.

Thus my first care must be to show that I had demanded her return because she mattered more to me than any other woman. I therefore commanded Maacah, whom I recognised as the only one among my wives whom Michal might see as a competitor, to return for the time being to her tribe: which she did, taking with her our two children, Absalom and Tamar. That I thus deprived myself, if only for the moment, of the company not only of that wife who most delighted me in love-making, but of the two children on whom I doted above all others, is proof of the sincerity of my ardour for Michal.

Joab said I was a fool to want her back.

"Woman's a bitch, and all that family's trouble. You ought to know that better than anyone, David. Still, nothing I can say'll make you shift your mind. You were always as besotted with her as Jonathan was with you."

Even faithful Laish raised doubts.

"Oh, I remember, David, how often I have heard you sigh for her, how you even sometimes" – he giggled – "called me by her name. But to revive the past? Can it be done? Is it even wise to try?"

But I waited for her, and remembered the deeds Saul had required me to perform in order to win her, and she approached, and the years fled. Her beauty was not altered, and she did not kneel when she approached me; and there was that old half-smile of mockery on her face when she said,

"So, David, my husband, and a king of sorts."

"One lacking his true queen."

"You could always make pretty speeches, which meant nothing, just as your singing could lure the King my father from his madness and from the devils which inhabited him – and that, alas, in the end, meant nothing either. But since you are a king – of sorts – and since I am your true wife whom you have required to return, here I am. Take me as I always was."

Which meant, as I knew and discovered again, in some sense apart from me even when we were most closely joined together.

15

Abner had proved his sincerity. Michal was restored to me, to my bed, and to my household, where she naturally assumed the chief place among my wives. I therefore now fixed a time and place to meet with Abner that we might deliberate how he could bring all Israel under my rule. To ease matters, and because I knew of the enmity Joab entertained for Abner, an enmity sharpened, I suspected, by the fear that Abner, by reason of his talents, his character, and the services he was about to perform for me, would rapidly supplant Joab and take the second place in my army and administration – for all these reasons, I now despatched Joab to quell some disturbances on the frontier with the Philistines, a task for which he was of course eminently fitted.

My negotiations with Abner could not have gone better. He confessed that he had blundered after the battle of Mount Gilboa when he had promoted the cause of Ishbosheth. But, he said, "I had promised Saul, in the extremity of his despair, that I would not betray his house, and so it seemed to me that I had no choice. Had I felt free in my mind and spirit to turn to you, David, I would have done so, for as you know I have always admired your talents and character. I never ceased to regret the hatred which Saul developed for you. But that hatred was a fact which loomed large in my considerations. Besides, I have to admit that there were many of the great men of Israel who had lost fathers, brothers, sons or other kindred at Mount Gilboa, who were warm against you on account of your association with the Philistines. 'If David had not allied himself to Achish,' they said, 'even though he did not himself take part in that dreadful battle, nevertheless the Philistines would have been weaker because they would have had to detach troops for the tasks which David's men were performing on their behalf; and therefore we might have gained the battle.' I am afraid, David," Abner continued, "that you may never have realised the damage which your association with the Philistines did you."

"And what choice had I?" I replied. "Was it not Saul who drove me into the wilderness where I might have starved like a wild beast had I not turned to Achish?"

Abner laid his hand on my knee.

"I have no doubt your judgement of what was necessary was sound. I don't know what I would have done had I found myself in your position. Believe me, I have every sympathy with you, and if you only knew how many countless times I tried to persuade Saul to abandon his war against you, well" – he threw up his hands – "it would be as easy to number the leaves on a tree or the grains of sand in the desert as to determine how often Jonathan and I spoke on your behalf. But that accursed visit of Samuel to your father's house in Bethlehem – that was a theme to which, again for reasons you cannot fail to understand, Saul always returned. It stuck like a fishbone in his gullet. Therefore we could not succeed. Nothing could prevail against Saul's hatred and fear of Samuel and your connection with the High Priest."

He drank some wine.

"David," he said, "I am only trying to explain why, even if I had not sworn to Saul that I would defend his house – and in that oath Saul read an undertaking that I would defy the memory and inheritance of Samuel – even if I had not done so, I could not have spoken up for you in Israel after the disaster of Mount Gilboa. The feeling against you was intense, not because men remembered how Saul persecuted you and approved of that persecution, but because of your alliance with Achish. Indeed, had I done so, I should only have weakened and perhaps even destroyed my own position and such influence as I possess."

"But now things are different?"

"Certainly. I have discussed these matters at length with

Achitophel, who has, as you know, a tenderness for you, and whom I have encouraged in the correspondence with you of which my agents long ago informed me. In the first place, time has passed, and the memory of your alliance with Achish has softened. Men are now readier to forgive it. Perhaps David had no choice, they say. In any case, the manner in which he has since conducted himself proves him no friend of the Philistines. Secondly, Ishbosheth's brutal stupidity has disgusted all. It has tarnished the memory of Saul. Saul, indeed, men say, was great and valiant in his youth, but Saul's character deteriorated with age and the long enjoyment of power. Ishbosheth cannot be compared with the glory of Saul in his youth, but he too shows signs of deterioration. The fact is that every day he disgusts the people more. Meanwhile, word comes that in Hebron David rules with patience and equity. Then there is talk of Samuel . . ."

"Yes," I said, "and what do men say of Samuel?"

"That he spoke the word of the Lord. That Ishbosheth's conduct is the manifestation of Samuel's wisdom in his understanding that the Lord had rejected the house of Saul. That perhaps men speak truth when they say that Samuel recognised David as the one who was truly the Chosen of the Lord, and therefore anointed him with oil."

"So at last," I said, "the time is ripe . . ."

"Indeed it is. Leave the matter in my hands, David."

"Willingly," I said, and embraced him.

And so it was arranged. Abner would return north and exercise his powers of persuasion on the chief men of the kingdom and the tribes, that they might agree to reject Ishbosheth, as the Lord had directed Samuel to reject Saul, and turn to me, as the True Lord's true Anointed. Seven years of patience, diplomacy, and restraint would in this way have their reward. My ambition would be fulfilled and the Lord's word be made manifest, and glorified.

But, alas, though I have ever trusted in the Lord, I have learned that Chance may undo the wisest and most virtuous of schemes. Chance, which I may also term contingency, plays a part in the affairs of men as dramatic as it is unfathomable.

It so happened that Joab despatched his business on the frontier with the efficiency I had expected but with an alacrity that I had not foreseen. He returned to Hebron just as Abner was departing. The report of his return had not reached me, for I was engaged with Maacah, whom I had secretly recalled and lodged in a house built within the eastern wall of Hebron; doing so, because I had found that Michal, despite the love I bore her and the devotion she still inspired in me, could not offer, by reason of the habit of disdainful reserve, increased by her ill-usage at the hand of Saul, could not or would not offer me that excitement of sensuality and that bliss of sexual release that Maacah invariably provided in her ardent and animal passion for my person.

I therefore lay with Maacah when desire was hot upon me and was in her arms when Joab returned and encountered Abner at the northern gate of the city.

Each, it was later reported to me, evinced surprise to see the other. The surprise was genuine on Abner's side, but it has since seemed probable that Joab, who maintained spies (as I suspected) even among the intimate servants of my household, had learned of Abner's mission and hastened to intercept him. Yet each pretended pleasure at the sight of the other. They fell on each other's necks and embraced. Then Joab suggested that to seal their reconciliation, and perhaps discuss other matters, they should retire for a little into a neighbouring tavern and drink wine as a symbol of past friendship and future good relations. Abner, noble and generous as ever, assented.

What transpired at first, what they talked of, in the little room of that dark tavern, can never be known with certainty. There may even have been no quarrel; but before the sun had shifted the angle at which it cast a shadow, Joab emerged, a bloody dagger in his hand, and cried out to Abishai that their brother Asahel was at last avenged. Then Joab's soldiers, as if prepared, fell upon Abner's little troop, slew some, and seized the others, bound their wrists and took them into custody in the military post manned by Joab's guards.

When the news was brought to me, I wept and tore my clothes, and called Joab to me.

He stood, stolid, sullen, and reproachful.

"David," he said, "what manner of man are you? You knew Abner as our enemy for many years, despite his protestations of friendship. You knew that without his aid Ishbosheth would never have been made King of Israel and that you would be king and I myself the second man in the kingdom as I am in Hebron. You knew him as the murderer of my brother Asahel, your nephew, whom you also loved. And yet, you send me to the frontier on a pretext, to do work of which a sergeant would be capable, and so, having contrived my absence, you invite our enemy here, and treat with him, and make much of him. David, no man has served you more loyally than I, Joab, and my brothers, the sons of Zeruiah. We deserted the service of Saul, in which we had won honour, for your sake; we risked death and dishonour for your sake; we chanced all for your sake; and you have rewarded us meanly. You have preferred Abner, the enemy of our house, and your enemy, for he clung to Saul and then set up Ishbosheth as king in your place – and yet you have preferred him to us, your most loyal servants. David, there is some perversity in you that makes you love your enemies and despise your friends. I remarked it in you from the first when I introduced you to glory by gaining you access to Saul; and yet you never thanked me, but turned from me and towards the King's son Jonathan, and lay with him while I raged in the dark outside. And now, when I have slain Abner, the enemy of our house and the murderer of my dearest brother, slain him in a fair fight that arose all of a sudden like the storms that break over the mountains of Judah, you reproach me and mourn him. David, this is unmanly, and unworthy of you. Consider only this. What has Abner done for you and what have I, Joab, done for you? Weigh these two questions and see which balance leaps up to kick the beam . . ."

The sincerity and the purity of his anger moved me, as Joab had never moved me before. I took him by the arm and led him out of the chamber and on to the terrace. Night was falling and the first stars and an infant moon were showing on the rim of the mountains of Judah of which he had spoken. Below, in the town, donkeys brayed and the girls were drawing water from the wells of evening.

"Joab," I said – and I infused my voice with all that tender sweetness with which I used to charm the maidens of Bethlehem when I sang to them in my youth – "Joab, if I have wronged you, forgive me. Even if I have not wronged you and you yet believe that I have done so, forgive me. I know and value your devotion to me, and I know and value your services more than words can tell. I too loved Asahel. I too mourned him, and still mourn him. But a king is not just a man. A king may not permit himself to feel only as a man feels. Word came to me of disaffection in the north. You yourself have formerly chided me for my decision to wait till I had such word, but would have had me march instead and seize the throne and drive the wretched Ishbosheth into exile. And yet when I argued my case, you had the grace to accede to it. Well then," I paused and placed my arm round his shoulders, "when word came, it came direct from Abner. He insisted on a meeting between us two. Yes, you are right, I thought it politic to send you off on what you describe as a sergeant's mission. I am sorry now. It would have been better if I had told you then what I am telling you now. But . . . if my meeting with Abner had not gone well . . . then I feared that in your righteous desire to avenge Asahel . . . what has happened would happen . . . Of course, if things went as I hoped, I planned to tell you as soon as you returned. Well, I tried to be too clever, too careful, and the blame is mine. I am sorry, Joab, truly sorry."

And I took him in my arms and felt his grizzled cheek rub against mine.

You may wonder, as many did then, that I did not punish Joab for the murder of Abner. There would have been advantages in doing so. Nothing would more completely have cleared me from suspicion of complicity in the eyes of the northern tribes and Abner's own extensive kinship. Moreover, the Law requires that a murderer be put to death – though I grant that there are differing interpretations when it is a question of revenge.

Yet all I did was suggest that he retire for a few months to the tranquil refuge of his father's house in Bethlehem.

Certainly I had been deeply moved by Joab's outburst, which made me aware that his feelings were more complicated and admirable than I had supposed; his character deeper, more complex, and more attractive. But I have ever been a man easily moved in such a manner, yet capable of cold action the following morning, action which may contradict the tenor of the emotion. It is, I suppose, what I have heard called "the artistic temperament".

There was another reason, which I am loth to confess. In my occupation with diplomacy and affairs of state, I had come to neglect the day-to-day management of the army. I had left that to Joab and I had left recruitment to him. I could not be certain therefore whether in a moment of crisis my troops would obey me, or their immediate master, Joab.

I gave Abner a magnificent funeral. The band of my royal guard played a lament of my own composition. I led the procession wearing only a simple robe of mourning, barefoot and with ashes on my head. At the graveside, I raised my voice and sang out:

> *Should Abner die as a fool dieth?*
> *Thy hands were not bound, nor thy feet put in fetters;*
> *As a man falleth before the children of iniquity,*
> *So didst thou fall.*

Then I decreed a day of fasting for the whole city, and when my herald came to urge me to break fast (as he had been ordered to do, where I sat in the public square), I spoke out and said: "Do you not know that there is a great prince fallen this day in Israel, and shall the King eat? I would rather the vultures picked the bones of Abner than that food should enter between my lips this awful day. Blessed be the Lord that commands mourning for such a prince as Abner, such a mighty man of valour, so wise in counsel, and politic in action. He came here as a peacemaker, we talked in amity, and now he is taken from us. Blessed be the Lord God of Hosts."

And so I made my grief manifest, and words of it passed to all the northern tribes and to the family of Abner in particular; and word came that their hearts warmed to me on account of my grief and the respect I had shown for their dead chief.

But I made no mention of his killer, for I saw no reason to stir up further and deeper animosity. If at any time the priests who record these matters ascribe to me words spoken or curses directed at Joab and the sons of Zeruiah, why, then, the scribes lie.

Yet I kept the memory of Joab's deed live in my heart.

My correspondence with the sage Achitophel assured me that opinion among the great men of the north was daily swinging in my direction, while the wretched Ishbosheth, conscious of his loss of esteem, and gripped by fears unworthy of a king, sank daily into the despicable habit of intoxication.

Now it so happened that at our last meeting I had inquired of Abner whether any of Jonathan's family still survived. There was one only: the lame boy, Mephibosheth, dropped by his nurse in terror on some occasion, and now kept at the court of his uncle the King as an object of ridicule and contempt.

I sent word by way of Achitophel that the boy would be welcome in Hebron. I did so not only because it pleased me in this way to repay, however inadequately, the debt I owed to my beloved Jonathan, but because I knew that word of such favour shown to the unfortunate child of the heroic son of Saul would do me credit among the tribe of Benjamin. And so Achitophel secured the lad's escape from the house of Ishbosheth, and had him led to Hebron by night stages in the charge of trusted guards.

The boy was timid, pale, thin-faced, small for his age, and clearly conscious of his paralysed arm and halting gait. But when he smiled there was the shadow of Jonathan's smile to be seen, and in repose his face had the look of Jonathan's in moments of perplexity. I called him to me, and bade him sit on my lap.

"Your father," I said, "was the best and truest friend I ever knew all the days of my life, and so, all those days that remain to me, you shall be welcome here, a safe and honoured guest in the house of David."

I stroked his hair and kissed him on the lips and set him down. He seized my hand and covered it with kisses. All around applauded and the boy blushed.

"Don't be afraid," I said. "And you will soon learn not to be shy."

*   *   *

Only one person was not delighted by my reception of the boy: Michal, his aunt.

"Why, David," she said, "do you choose to humiliate me? You protest that you love me more than any other woman, that I am the pearl or ruby among your wives, and yet you expose me to this public insult. You know that, through no fault of mine, but by the Lord's will and perhaps on account of my father's treatment of me, I cannot conceive a child. Naturally the other women of your household – some of them the most wretched and common creatures – remark on this, though not of course in my presence. But now you have brought this cripple here, whom they know to be my brother's son, and so they can point at him and say: 'If she had had a child it would be a monster like that.' Do you think of what you are doing, David? Is the desire for popularity all that dominates you? Do you ever consider my feelings?"

"But the boy is not a cripple from birth. His nurse dropped him on the ground when he was a baby. That is why he is as he is. And he is Jonathan's son."

"Don't talk to me of Jonathan whom you stole from me."

"What do you mean?"

"Really, David, I sometimes think you are no different from the shepherd-boy I first met stinking of sheep and goats."

16

Happily, the honour I did Abner, the report of my anger with Joab, and of my reception of Jonathan's son, achieved the effect which I sought. Almost daily I received emissaries from the north urging me to muster my forces and remove the intolerable Ishbosheth. Still I delayed, waiting for the ripe fruit to fall from the tree. At night I stood under the heavens on the roof of my little palace and gazed north as the moon rose above the mountains and the silence of night was broken by the barking of dogs and the howls of the desert jackals. I prayed to the Lord that he would give me a sign.

But none came, none that I could certainly recognise; and so I waited.

Meanwhile, every report I received indicated that support was slipping from Ishbosheth as a cup of water disappears in the sands of the wilderness.

His end was sudden and brutal. Two unruly men, Rechab and Naanan, the sons of Rimmon, a Beerothite, entered the King's palace on some pretext, made their way to his bedchamber and found him lying there drunk from the night's debauch, though it was now noon. They stabbed him with their daggers, and then cut off his head, and escaped the palace, the guards being indolent or indifferent to their duty. They then travelled south and presented themselves to me in Hebron and drew the blood-encrusted head of Ishbosheth from the bag in which they were carrying it; and showed it to me, and smiled.

And one said, "David, behold the head of your enemy, the son of Saul who sentenced you to death. Israel is yours, my lord."

And the other said: "It was the Lord's will. We have done what we have done at the command of the Lord of Hosts who, by way of Samuel, anointed you with oil."

They smiled as they knelt before me, expecting me to be pleased, and to reward them. But I shrank back in horror from these men of blood.

Now let me be honest. Why not? I am too old to lie.

I was of course pleased that Ishbosheth had been removed, for I knew that this ensured that the chief men of all the tribes of Israel would now summon me to be king, and that I would assume the throne without a war which would set Israelite to slay Israelite. So in my heart I was glad; and I knew that this was indeed the sign which I had sought from the Lord.

Yet I was also wretched, to see the look on the faces of the murderers as they laid the head of Ishbosheth at my feet. And I knew that to reward regicide was to endanger my own position in future. No state can be secure in which the life of the King is not regarded as sacrosanct.

So I said to them, speaking in a loud voice, that all those gathered around might hear:

"When, after the battle of Mount Gilboa, a fool brought me the head of Saul thinking thus to please me, how did I reward him? Now you bring me the head of his son that was also king in Israel and expect me to reward you for having murdered a man as he lay in his own bed. You shall have the same reward that I gave to the Amalekite who brought me the gift of Saul's head."

I called my guard and put the men under arrest, and judged them, as they deserved. The guards cut them down before my eyes, and cut off their hands and their feet, and hung them for a warning to all over the pool in Hebron.

I then had the head of Ishbosheth entombed in the sepulchre I had built for Abner. If Abner had lived, we would have disposed of Ishbosheth in a more seemly manner. It would have been sufficient to put out his eyes and then compel him to live out his life in the charge of the priests of the Most High.

With Ishbosheth's murder my inheritance was secure, for the punishment I had dealt out to his murderers convinced all those still loyal to the house of Saul that I had had no hand in his death, as was indeed the case.

Few dared to remark that the sons of Rimmon had earlier served in the special forces which Joab had recruited and trained as frontier guards.

And so the promise made to me by the Lord, through the mouth of Samuel, was fulfilled, and in my thirtieth year I became King of All-Israel, amidst general rejoicing.

I now determined to embark on a scheme which had been in my mind for years, ever since that first evening when, travelling with Joab to Saul's palace to cure the King of his madness, we had seen the lights of Jerusalem twinkling across the valley. Then, it may be recalled, I had asked Joab why we suffered the Jebusites to retain control of a city which, it seemed, had been designed by nature and the Lord to be the chief place in Israel. That thought had recurred to me often throughout the years of struggle, and now, when I was wondering where I should fix my chief residence, I turned my face to Jerusalem again.

I would be sorry of course to leave Hebron, where I had lived happily, and been held in honour, for seven years; but Hebron was not only the stronghold of my own tribe of Judah, which in itself made it unsuitable as my principal residence if I was to retain the loyalty, so recently won, of the northern tribes; but being also situated in the extreme south of the land of Israel, it was ill-placed if I was to exercise effective government over the whole land, especially since communications between north and south were interrupted by the Jebusites' possession of Jerusalem and the surrounding country.

Saul had resided chiefly in Gibeah, where Ishbosheth had been murdered, but Gibeah was the city of the tribe of Benjamin, and I feared that to choose Gibeah would be resented by Judah.

Shiloh had long been the holy place of Israel; it was there that the priests had guarded the Ark of the Covenant till that moment of disgrace when it was taken by the Philistines and removed to Gath. It was at Shiloh that Samuel had ministered to the old High Priest Eli, and it was still held to be a holy place. But since it was sacked by the Philistines, its walls had never been fully repaired;

and in any case, though I have always found it prudent to show reverence to the priests, I did not wish to do anything that might recall to men the days when Israel was ruled by the Judges and the High Priest rather than by a king.

Moreover, Shiloh was in the land of Ephraim, and, to some extent, the same objection held good in regard to Shiloh as to Hebron and Gibeah. I was determined to be King of All-Israel, to weld the twelve tribes into a powerful and coherent nation-state, and I realised that the more closely they associated me with any one tribe, the more difficult this task would be to accomplish.

For all these reasons Jerusalem seemed to me to be the ideal city in which to establish my residence; I therefore announced that it was the will of the Lord that Jerusalem should fall into the hands of Israel, that it might be the capital and City of David.

It also seemed good to me to perform some act at the very beginning of my reign which would impress all the tribes with my greatness. Kings live and flourish according to their authority, as well as their power, and authority depends on esteem, as power depends on the ability to arouse fear. I had no doubt that I possessed power, but I sought the authority that a brilliant action, appealing to the imagination of all, could win me; and therefore within a few weeks of being acknowledged King of All-Israel, I instructed Joab to prepare plans for an assault on Jerusalem.

He was doubtful at first, though he understood my reasons.

"They are good reasons," he said, scratching his long nose, "persuasive reasons, David. Yet . . ." he paused still scratching his nose, ". . . if we should fail . . . and we may fail, for Jerusalem is so well fortified that the Jebusites have a proverb that the blind and the lame are sufficient for its defence – if we should fail, then the blow to your authority and power would be one from which you would find it hard to recover."

"Well, Joab," I replied, "your advice is as usual good. And indeed I wish I had consulted you sooner, for if I had, you might have persuaded me, as you are, as you know, capable of doing. But most unfortunately, in a moment of what I admit to be rashness, I have already announced that it is the Lord's will that we take Jerusalem and that it be known as the City of David. This being so, you will realise that to draw back is impossible."

Joab scratched his nose again, and reluctantly agreed. It had been, of course, in anticipation of his objections that I had made my public announcement.

"Joab," I spoke now in a gentle tone, "I know you have thought deeply of how this might be done, and I recall – from those many years ago – how you suggested that the city might be taken if you divided your army, and pretended that the main assault was to be launched from the south, so as to draw the defenders away from the northern walls, which are less well protected by nature, and then, when those defences have been further weakened in this manner, you would make a fierce assault with the main body of the army from that side."

"I remember that was my plan," Joab said.

"It was your plan," I said, "and therefore I entrust to you the management of the attack, that you may have the honour and the glory of being both the author and executioner. Only bear this in mind. When the city has been taken, I wish to spare the Jebusites. It will be useful to us to have a city populated by those who owe everything, even their lives, to us, and who have no friends in Israel except the King and his noble general."

Joab saw my point. He would not have thought of it himself, and, left to his own devices, would have permitted his soldiers to indulge themselves in an orgy of blood; but when the matter was made clear to him, he understood very well the wisdom of what I suggested.

As a matter of fact I had no clear memory of whatever plan Joab had suggested in the course of that distant conversation. It may indeed have resembled that which I now advanced to him.

"The Lord of Hosts be with you," I said.

All went as I had intended. The city which boasted such secure defences fell to us at little cost. When the Jebusites heard that their lives and property were to be spared, they were astonished, and greeted me as a deliverer rather than their conqueror.

So, I won my capital city, and immediately set myself to

reordering the State. At the same time I determined to build myself a palace worthy of a great king, and for this purpose opened negotiations with Hiram, King of Tyre. I had as a young man been impressed by what seemed to me the superior civilisation of the Philistines, and their achievements in the art of building. But during my time at the court of my friend Achish, I had learned that the Philistines were themselves inferior in this respect to the Phoenician people of Tyre and Sidon; and even Achish confessed to me that, proud as he was of his own people, their finest buildings were but base imitations of what the Phoenicians had achieved.

I therefore sent Achitophel, as the man of the subtlest intelligence in my employ, to Tyre to propose an alliance with King Hiram. It is true that there was little I could offer in exchange for what I hoped to receive from him. But in conversation with Achitophel we agreed on the means of winning his friendship.

The Phoenicians are a people more given to trade than warfare; and like all who have prospered and learned the pleasures of luxury, they fear men who have lived rough and who, never having experienced comfort, despise those who lead soft and luxurious lives. Achitophel was to impress upon King Hiram that we Israelites were such a people. He was even to malign my character and to portray me as a man who had waded through blood to a throne, who rejoiced in warfare, and whom a prudent and pacific monarch would rather have as ally than enemy. Moreover, Achitophel was to say: "East of Jordan are tribes still more wild than the twelve tribes of Israel, which David has united and formed into a mighty armed nation. These tribes beyond Jordan lust after the spoils of Tyre and Sidon, but between them and you stands David who seeks your friendship. If you grant it him, he will serve as a bulwark and sure defence against the fierce and greedy tribes of the desert. But if you deny it, then David is swift to anger, and it will be hard for a man of peace like myself to control him. He will be tempted to listen to his men of war like Joab and Abishai, the sons of Zeruiah, and to put himself at the head of the savage tribes of the desert and launch a mighty army against you."

Hiram, being an intelligent man, preferred peace and friendship to the certain dangers and uncertain outcome of war. He therefore quickly agreed to make a treaty with me, and in return for the security I offered him, to furnish me with the skilled craftsmen and materials I required in order to fulfil my dream of building myself a palace, for I desired to surround myself with visible beauty and splendour equal to what I could myself achieve in the arts of poetry and music.

So the next year was spent in watching the building of my palace, happy in the knowledge that in creating it, I was not only bringing a new splendour to Israel, but impressing myself on the nation as a king superior in glory and magnificence to poor Saul who had lived (as I now saw) rudely. It amused me to think, as daily I saw my dream realised, how I had been impressed by Saul's palace in my ignorant and innocent youth.

It was my desire to live at peace with my neighbours, but my achievement aroused their jealousy and fear. I believed I had no quarrel with the Philistines, and I retained a warm memory of the kindness which Achish had shown me. But Achish was now dead, and the new kings of the Philistines were dismayed to see how my power and reputation grew. Provoked only by this, they gathered a great army and invaded the land of Israel. I was therefore compelled to resume the military life which I hoped, for the Lord's honour and glory, to have put behind me.

I drew up my army in the Valley of Rephaim, south of Jerusalem, and awaited the onslaught. As they approached I withdrew before them, apparently towards the city, as if, dismayed by the size of their forces, I had resolved to retire within its walls and stand a siege. Using the dead ground of the little valley, however, I changed the direction of our march, so that I manoeuvred my forces to the flank of the enemy where we lay concealed in a wood of mulberry trees.

There was, despite my reluctance, a pleasure in being once again in the field, pitting my wits against the enemy. From my long experience of irregular warfare I had learned to know the country and to observe the moods and habits of the weather. I knew that in that valley a little breeze rose up just before the sun sank beneath the hills and that the sound of the wind in the mulberry trees resembled the march of a mighty army. I told my soldiers that before the sun went down, the Lord would send an invisible force to our aid; and that the signal for our attack on the Philistines would be the sound of its marching feet. We lay in the shade of the trees through the heat of the afternoon while I watched the army of the Philistines advance in column over the hill and descend into the valley that would lead them to Jerusalem. They marched like men determined to finish a job. Three times only a trumpet sounded as if to encourage them. But there was silence as the sun sank and the dust rose from the column passing before us. Then, as I had foretold, the little breeze blew up. It shook the trees and the leaves rattled . . .

"The Lord of Hosts has come to our aid," I cried, and we fell upon the flank of the Philistines. Surprise was complete. They had no time to range themselves in battle order. We scattered them like the leaves of autumn, and they fled before us in terror and confusion. The pursuit lasted till the moon was up; and the army of Philistia was no more.

I would fight other wars against Edom and Moab and triumph there also, but this victory over the Philistines in the Valley of Rephaim was the greatest of my career. The Philistines had oppressed Israel for many generations, since the days of the Judges. The mighty Samson had struggled against them. They had subdued and plundered Israel in the days of Eli. Saul had battled bravely against them till he was overwhelmed on Mount Gilboa. But never again. I broke the power of the Philistines in the Valley of Rephaim as the wind shook the mulberry trees, broke it in fragments like a shattered pot, and compelled them to sue for peace in more humble terms than ever before.

I imposed severe conditions, compelling the Philistines to dismantle their fortified places, and to accept my authority over them. I recruited some of their bravest fighting men into my personal bodyguard, both to do them honour and show myself fearless and magnanimous; and also because I had concluded that a bodyguard composed largely of foreigners would be a more secure defence for me than one drawn from the jealous tribes of Israel. And, most important of all, I required them to deliver the Ark of the Covenant which they had taken from Israel in the days of Eli; and so I brought the Lord's dwelling-place back to the Lord's own land of Israel.

17

In the dewy glory of a summer dawn I brought the Ark of the Covenant to Jerusalem.

The mist still hung around the fringes of the olive trees and the sun was still obscured when the Ark was brought from the house of Obededom, a Levite, where it had rested three months while I prepared its entry to my city which is also the Lord's. And when the priests brought it forth and placed it with due reverence on an ox-wagon, I threw myself on the ground, and worshipped the spirit of the Lord of Hosts.

Then sacrifices were performed, according to the Law, and seven companies of singers were assembled to march before the Ark praising the Lord as we climbed the hill towards Jerusalem. As the procession began to move, the sun broke through the dissolving clouds and a shout was raised that the Lord was pleased.

I walked, alone, behind the last company of the singers, and played the small harp, and the music was of my own composition. So we advanced towards Jerusalem and the crowd grew greater as we neared the city. They pressed forward to view the Ark, and they cast flowers among us. A little girl broke from the throng and placed a garland of flowers about my neck.

Now in the square or open space before my palace I had caused a great tabernacle to be erected to receive the Ark, and as we approached it, I raised my voice and sang:

The earth is the Lord's and the fullness thereof;
The world and they that dwell therein;
For He hath founded it upon the seas
And established it upon the floods."

Then a choir of youths, with voices unbroken, who stood arrayed in white tunics of fine linen before the tabernacle, sang the challenge:

Who shall ascend into the hill of the Lord?
And who shall stand in His holy place?

There was silence, as I had commanded, that the full import of the question be understood, and then the priests, their gaze fixed upon me, replied:

He that hath clean hands and a pure heart;
Who hath not lifted up his soul unto vanity,
Nor sworn deceitfully.
He shall receive the blessing of the Lord
And righteousness from the God of his salvation.

Now the whole company of singers sang:

This is the generation of them that seek Him,
That seek thy face, O Jacob.

The trumpets sounded and the cymbals clanged, and the whole multitude of Israel there assembled opened their hearts to welcome the return of the Ark:

Lift up your heads, O ye gates,
And be ye lift up, ye everlasting doors;
And the King of Glory shall come in!

But again the choir of boys, with all instruments of music stilled, sang the question:

Who is this King of Glory?

And I myself answered:

The Lord strong and mighty, the Lord mighty in battle.

The whole company took up the song:

Lift up your heads, O ye gates,
Even lift them up, ye everlasting doors,
And the King of Glory shall come in.
Who is this King of Glory?
The Lord of Hosts, mighty in battle,
He is the King of Glory.

I laid my harp aside, and advancing into the centre of the open space before the tabernacle, mounted on a plinth, and spoke to the people. I spoke in a low voice, and yet my words were heard by all, and echoed to the surrounding hills.

"When our forefathers were in the wilderness after they had escaped the tyranny of Egypt, the Lord made a covenant with Moses and with all the Children of Israel, that this land of Israel should be ours for all succeeding generations. And the Ark, the abode of the Lord, marked that covenant.

"Then in the dark days of Israel, in the time of Eli the High Priest, the Philistines made cruel war on Israel, and laid impious hands on the Ark of the Covenant, and carried it away to their own cities, that Israel might fear that the the Lord had turned his back on his people. And when the Ark was taken from us in this manner darkness fell on the land, a deep darkness as of a winter night. But still the Children of Israel trusted in the Lord of Hosts, and the Lord continued to watch over us. The great King Saul struggled against the Philistines, and in his service a mere shepherd-boy, by the Grace of the Lord of Hosts, slew the champion of the Philistines, the giant Goliath.

"But still the Ark was kept from us.

"Samuel had anointed that shepherd-boy with oil to signify that he was the Chosen of the Lord, and when Saul, mighty in battle, was cruelly slain, that shepherd-boy, even I myself, became king in his place. In many battles with the aid of my noble soldiers and the blessing and strong arm of the Lord of Hosts, I defeated the Philistines and drove them out of Israel, even to the gates of Gath. And I compelled them to submit to me, to the will of Israel, and of the Lord of Hosts. So they surrendered the Ark of the Covenant, which this day we restore to the glory

of the Lord in this city of Jerusalem which from this day on shall
be a holy place."

Saying these words, I let my kingly robe slip from me, and fall
to the ground, and I stood naked before all the people, save for a
loin-cloth of yellow linen, as if I was the humblest of the priests
of the Lord. Then I gave a sign and the musicians played, and I
began to dance.

I cannot recall that dance; I could never have repeated it. My
first steps, I think, were slow, even, it seemed, uncertain, as if I
was aware of my temerity in stripping my soul in the sight of
the Lord.

What is Man, the dance said, that Thou art mindful of him,
and as the steps of the dance put this greatest of questions, I
bent my body first back, then forward, so that the hair of my
head touched the dust of the earth. It seemed, I remember, as
if I stood outside myself, and witnessed the movements of this
body which had become the servant of the dance of the Lord.

Then the music quickened and the dance grew wilder as it
spoke of the greatness and grace of the Lord's creation, of His
gifts to Israel and the great kindness He had done us. I paused, at a
still moment between the changing rhythms, and drew my arms
across my body, seeming to shrink before the majesty and terror
of the Lord; and then the dance again took wild possession of the
dancer as it spoke of the Lord, mighty in battle, whose servant
in the destruction of the enemies of Israel the dancer was.

And all the time the congregation of the people stood silent
and still as the stars of winter, but all were held rapt as a lover
who beholds the beauty of his love.

The music stopped as dance and dancer fell to the earth,
humble before the Ark; and from that position, feeling the
warm grit of the soil against my naked flesh, I raised my head
and, without accompaniment sang that psalm I had made for
Saul in his madness:

The Lord is my shepherd; I shall not want . . .

When I came to the last line: "and I will dwell in the house
of the Lord for ever", a shiver of recognition ran through the
congregation of the people and we were all joined together as

one body, one soul, united in wonder and awe of the majesty and goodness of the Almighty.

In that moment I was truly wed to my people, and I held that silence longer than it would take a man to fit an arrow to a bow and let it fly to the heart of his target. I held it longer yet, until the trembling of my limbs was stilled, and the racing of my heart subsided. Then I threw myself prostrate before the Ark, and pressed my body to the earth while the priests sang their prayer of thanks to the Almighty. And when I rose, I wiped the sweat from my brow with my forearm.

I had done all that which I had sought to do, and I knew my triumph was absolute. But I knew also that it was necessary to lead the congregation from the heights of exultation to which I had raised them, for a large crowd in such a condition is an incalculable thing. So it seemed good to me to guide the people to the plains of common experience, so that the intensity of the ceremonies might be succeeded by a mood of happy holiday. I had therefore arranged that a public feast should be prepared, and myself oversaw the distribution of bread, meat, a raisin cake and wine to each person present. Then, when all were happily engaged in feasting, I withdrew into my palace.

The day was past its zenith and I still rested, while the sounds of revelry rose to me from the city below. I was conscious, I remember, of a profound peace, a happiness that came from my understanding that I had that day excelled myself, that, to the glory of the Almighty, I had created in the ceremony a perfect work of art.

I sent for one of my concubines – I forget which – and lay with her so that we were as one flesh, and then dismissed her, and slept.

When I woke, the light was fading, and a servant entered my chamber with a lamp, and informed me that the lady Michal wished to speak with me. Before I could give my assent, the curtain was brushed aside, and Michal was with me. She stood over my couch, and in the shadowy light the angular beauty of her face was softened, and I felt a desire for her which I had not known for many months. I stretched out my arms, and then she spat in my face.

"Showman," she said, "buffoon. What have I done to be so humiliated?"

I thought: she is angry because I summoned that concubine to my bed instead of her, in my day of triumph. But then, surely she realises that I would never treat her as a thing to be summoned to satisfy my needs. I thought: doesn't she realise that my love for her is of a different kind? A different nature? I wanted to say all this, but before I could speak, she stripped the covers off me to reveal my nakedness.

"You have disgraced me," she said, and her voice was cold as the desert nights, "you have humiliated me before all the people. That you, a king, should dance naked before the young girls of the city, yes, even before the whores! How could you? Have you no self-respect? Do you suppose my father, King Saul, would have exposed himself to the people, and trailed his head in the dust like a fool or a madman?"

I thought: she does not understand me. She has never understood me. She has no sense of what we owe the Almighty. I thought: and I have been wrong myself. I took her for a creature set apart from the common run, someone possessed of sublimity, whose beauty of person mirrored the beauty of her soul. And I have deceived myself, cheated myself.

I thought: it is in this respect that I have been a fool.

But still I did not reply to her, for I could think of no words that would not be harsh, and none that would not express the sadness I now felt when I looked at her. Even as I did so it seemed that time, disappointment, and contempt had corrupted even her beauty.

"How glorious you were," she said, "what a wonderful sight to see the King writhing naked in the dust!"

"Michal," I said, "I danced before the Lord to do honour to His holy name who chose me as King of Israel when he rejected your father Saul. If you think it disgraceful or contemptible to humble myself before the Lord, then I am sorry for you. Let me tell you, even the poor girls of the city – yes, and the whores also – understood what I was doing today. They were in tune with my dance, because however wretched they may be in their daily lives, they caught today a glimmer of the majesty of the Almighty. But you, shut up in palaces, and despising the people, despise also the Almighty if you despise me, His servant. It makes me wretched to see you locked up in your pride and selfishness and ignorance, so that you cannot . . ." I spread my hands when I saw her frozen and uncomprehending face.

"Words," she said, "words. You can always find words to justify whatever you do, David. You use words to escape me, David, always have. You jump and slide sideways, and then disappear, and yet all the time you insist that the light shines on you and even that you yourself are the cause of light."

I thought: what she is saying may indeed be true, but it is not related to what she says has aroused her anger. She has lived with me as the wife I most loved and yet she does not know me, because she has never wanted to know me. Perhaps she has never loved me. Perhaps she is incapable of love and this is why we have made no child.

And then I thought: but I have been a fool myself. I have been able to love her, to say I love her, and to have been sure that was true, only perhaps because I myself have declined to know her, and have persuaded myself that she is what I wanted her to be and not what she truly is. Whatever that is. Perhaps it really is the narrow, life-denying, God-denying thing that appears before me now.

This thought made me sad, but I was also angry. I rose from my couch, and stood before her. We were the same height and I looked into her eyes, those dark pools which I had found so mysterious and delightful, and I said:

"Yes, Michal, it may be that the whores of the city are dearer to the Lord than you are, for they do not deny him in their hearts."

"You thing," she said, "you play-actor," and turned and left the apartment.

I drank wine from the jug and found that I was trembling. We had had many quarrels over the years which had usually ended in love-making. But this could not end like that. I saw that. I thought: we have really come to the end. And I am not sure if I am distressed. We are like people separating on a journey, and there is nothing that can be done about it.

I gave orders that Michal was to be treated with all honour and courtesy, but confined to her own apartments – till, I thought, I could establish her in a residence of her own – and denied access to mine or to my person.

When I rejected Michal and commanded that she be excluded from my presence, the cold breath of winter was laid upon me. I had given everything I might to Michal; the greatest of my exploits were performed for her sake. In exile, in the long nights of the wilderness, her beauty had come to me in dreams, and there were bedmates who had wept when I woke with Michal's name on my lips.

Now I thought: she was only an ordinary woman. The Michal of my dreams I had invented for myself. And the thought pained me. I had supposed my house built upon a rock, and I learned that its foundations were shifting as the sands of the desert.

Something in me was now broken, and has never been repaired. For months I took no pleasure in women, and my other wives and concubines reproached my lack of interest with lowered eyes and lashes damp with tears.

For consolation I threw myself still more energetically into the task for which the Almighty had chosen me: to form the tribes of Israel into a powerful nation and coherent state. I laboured long hours; dawn often touched the sky with pink before the lamp in my study-chamber was extinguished.

In the time of Saul, responsibilities for the administration and government of the people were allotted in a casual and haphazard manner – poor Saul had no understanding of method. In his day the effects were not calamitous, for the King's household was small, his authority weak, and the scope of government limited. Indeed, to tell truth, I had come to see that Saul, whom I had feared and served with reverence in my youth, was no more than a tribal war-leader. He commanded the host, but among the people, the leaders of the tribes and the headmen of the villages ordered affairs. And in the matter of the Law the priests' writ still ran, sometimes in uneasy association with custom.

Now I saw that this would not do. For one thing, as king, I now ruled over more than the Children of Israel; my subjects included many from other tribes, and it was necessary that I regulate relations between them and impose some measure of uniformity. In pursuit of this I was greatly aided by the sagacity of Achitophel, who came closer to a full understanding of my aims than any other man – whatever cause I subsequently had to reproach Achitophel, I have never concealed my admiration for his intelligence. I was also helped by Hushai the Archite who had entered my service as a clerk, but whom I soon promoted on account of his evident intelligence. Hushai, being slight of stature and somewhat lame in his left leg, was no soldier, and for this reason despised by Joab; but considering him, I thought: what I am trying to create requires all types of talent, and a man who lacks the military virtues may nevertheless be useful. I was proved right in my judgement for Hushai's advice was acute, and, being nearer to my sons than to myself in age, he was able to keep me informed as to the feelings among the younger men. I have often observed how kingdoms decline as the King ages.

One of my principal concerns was to strengthen the army, for Israel was surrounded by jealous and hostile neighbours. I recruited a crack brigade of guards – a *corps d'élite*, as the Syrians put it. One battalion was always attached to my own person, to serve as the royal bodyguard, while the other served with the main body of the army, at the point of greatest danger. The two battalions exchanged duties every half-year; and in this way I ensured that they all stood in a personal relationship to me, and indeed each guardsman was required to take an oath of loyalty to the King rather than to Israel. Many were recruited from tribes beyond our borders, especially from among the Philistines, and I was always ready to admit foreigners from more distant lands to the corps. I remained acutely conscious of the rivalries and jealousies that divided Israel; therefore, I valued my guards who were free from tribal loyalties and who served only me. They enlisted for a period of twenty years, whereas the main body of the army consisted of short-term conscripts.

Maintaining such a force was expensive, and I gave close attention to the reform of the administrative system necessary to secure the payment of taxes on a regular and satisfactory basis. I knew this could not be popular, but, believing it to be necessary, did not shrink from the task, and trusted that my reputation and natural authority would be sufficient to secure the not altogether reluctant obedience of my subjects. Moreover, I was anxious to accumulate treasure in order that I might in time build a temple worthy of the greatness of the Lord of Hosts.

The commander of the guard was Benaiah, of my own tribe of Judah, a man of the utmost integrity. It did not entirely displease me to discover that Joab disliked him, and that Benaiah had no warm feelings for my second-in-command. In any case Joab had wished the command of the guard to go to his brother Abishai. But I preferred Benaiah. Many of the guardsmen, as I have said, were Philistines, and Abishai retained his old prejudice against their nation. This alone would have made him an unsuitable commander – even if there had been no other consideration.

Since I have mentioned my purpose of accumulating treasure in order to build a house worthy of the Lord, it seems good to me to give the lie to certain stories which I am told have been put about concerning this matter.

It is said that when I broached my intention to Nathan the prophet, he reproved me in the name of the Lord, and told me that my purpose was offensive to the Almighty. This is of course just the sort of story which men like to believe. Apparently, Nathan – for whom I have always incidentally had the highest esteem – told me, first, that the Lord preferred to dwell in a tent rather than in a house made of cedarwood; and second, that the Lord had rejected me as the builder of His temple because I was a man of war, stained with blood. The fact that these two contradictory stories are told as if they were consistent with each other should be enough to call both into question.

It is true, certainly, that Nathan, as an itinerant prophet, disliked the scheme; on the other hand, the priestly caste of Levites, of whom my old friend Abiathar was now chief, were enthusiastic supporters of my ambition, and had no doubt that the Lord would welcome the building of a temple that would bear witness to His glory. As for the charge that I was a man of blood, it was absurd; all my wars were fought in the name of the Most High.

The fact of the matter is that building a temple is a huge and expensive undertaking. I had no wish to leave my heir with a load of debt. Therefore I determined that I should not start building until I had accumulated sufficient treasure to finance the scheme. Now that I have done so, I am too old and lacking in energy to embark on an enterprise of which it is certain I could not live to see the conclusion. I have therefore entrusted the task to Solomon. He will perform it admirably, for he has inherited excellent taste from his mother as well as from myself. He should be grateful to me for the long and patient accumulation of wealth which will make it possible for him to do the job without bleeding his people and sacrificing his popularity. But his chilly soul is incapable of so generous an emotion as gratitude; and he will not in any case wish to acknowledge the debt he owes me.

No king should seek popularity, however, though he may be happy to be rewarded by it. If he wins it, he should beware. Our people are fickle, and popularity is fleeting. I myself have suffered vicissitudes of fortune and conspiracies against my life. Fortunately, thanks to the efficiency of my secret service, the management of which I entrusted to Achitophel, I have survived them.

I have survived also more than a hundred battles, thanks be to the Lord. I destroyed the power of the Philistines. I subdued the kingdom of Moab. I triumphed over Edom and Syria. I made my name feared throughout the world. I secured the frontiers of Israel and drove my enemies before me as the wind blows the sands of the desert. No one before me rendered the name of Israel a fearful word among the nations of the earth.

I endured and overcame treachery. When Nahash, King of Ammon, died, I sent envoys to his son Hanun, to assure him that I would continue firm in friendship to him as I had been to his father. The young man was rash and resentful of my greatness, which had indeed so impressed Nahash that he had submitted to me as his overlord. His son received my ambassadors with insults and defiance: he cut their beards and rent their garments to display their genitals. Then he formed an alliance with the wild tribes of the Syrians from beyond the great River Euphrates, and made war on Israel. By my advice Joab divided our forces, drove Hanun into his city of Rabbah, scattered the Syrian tribes, and gave siege to the city. It was strongly fortified, and the siege was long and arduous, but I was calm, for I had no doubts of our eventual success.

I took no direct part in this war, being content to direct its course from Jerusalem. I had grown weary of war, and sought delight in other things. But, since I had rejected Michal, I knew no delight. My life had fallen into an autumn mood, and only the unremitting attention I gave to the business of government served to conceal from me the pain I felt, restrained me from despair. Even my gift for poetry had dried up; and I felt myself to a withered husk. I looked to the stars and found them obscured by heavy clouds.

In the hot nights of early summer I could not sleep. During the day I was assailed by an unaccustomed lassitude, and felt myself perpetually weary. Yet when I retired to my chamber sleep was denied me. Formerly I would have summoned a concubine, or in still earlier days Laish or another boy; now I felt no inclination towards what had once been pleasures, but which, I now sensed, would bring me neither relief nor satisfaction.

I had achieved glory before all men, and found favour in the sight of the Lord; and I was bored and weary of all things, even my position.

I could not pray. I could not compose music or poetry.

Sometimes I recalled the nights of my youth when I had watched over our flocks in the hills above Bethlehem. What I missed now was what I had felt so keenly then: the eagerness of my body and the alertness of my soul's imagination. I looked over the rooftops of Jerusalem and asked myself why the people slept while the King could not.

One night I was especially perturbed. I had had that day an acrimonious conversation with Achitophel who had reported to me that his agents had told him of congress between my eldest son Amnon and certain kings of the Philistines.

"Who gave you authority to set your spies on my son?"

"My lord king," he replied, "it is for the security of Israel that I act."

But I did not believe him, suspecting that for purposes of his own, he wished to set me against Amnon who had never liked him.

I said: "Amnon is a boy of difficult and uncertain temperament, but he loves me, and is loyal. I wish to hear no more of this matter, and I order you to withdraw the spies you have set about him."

"Very well, my lord king," he replied, but I heard a note of irony in his voice, and could not be certain that he would obey me. And yet I dared not dismiss him, for I knew that he had used his position to win himself many friends and dependents; indeed I felt myself encompassed by those who owed loyalty to Achitophel rather than to myself, David the King. And I knew that he had been especially active building up his clientele among the young men of the court and the army. I feared that he had set them against Amnon; and yet I felt myself powerless to act against Achitophel, as I was in like manner powerless to act against Joab.

Then, when I had sent him away, I found myself wondering whether the news he brought me about Amnon's dealings with the Philistines might not be true. I loved Amnon, my firstborn, the child of Ahinoam in the days when I was not yet king, but a fugitive from Saul's jealousy. Perhaps because his childhood had been so disturbed and dangerous, he had grown up without that confidence I have always felt, and which was so manifest in his younger and more beautiful brother Absalom, the son of Maacah. I knew Amnon to be jealous of Absalom and I feared that he believed, against all reason and evidence, that I preferred his younger brother. So, although I had given Amnon every sign of my love and favour, he could not believe in its reality, for he could not believe in himself.

Thus I could not entirely dismiss the reports of Achitophel's spies, and yet I found them intolerable, and resented the knowledge which Achitophel claimed. I was perplexed and disturbed and my soul was heavy with foreboding.

In this mood of dissatisfaction, I rose from my sleepless couch and walked on to the terrace that opened out of my bedchamber. The air was warm and the moon rose high above the city; yet I could not feel the glory of the Lord. I leaned on the parapet, and thought I had never been so lonely in my life, for in the nights of my youth in the hills above Bethlehem I had ever been conscious of the glorious future that awaited me; and now it was all dust and ashes and dismay.

Then a figure moved on one of the rooftops of the houses below the palace. It was a woman. Unconscious of my presence, she disrobed and began to sponge her body, dipping the sponge into a basin and then letting the cool water flow over her. For a moment I watched her with only idle curiosity, and then as she bent again to the basin the wandering moon lit upon her, and I caught my breath; never, I knew, had I seen such graceful movement, such a perfection of form. Her hair fell over her breasts and she threw her head back and the tresses fell behind her and she sponged her breasts; then, leaning forward again, sponged between her legs. And desire rose in me, and it was as if I could taste the damp softness of her flesh.

Still unconscious that I was watching her – now with an urgency that it seemed impossible should not be communicated to her, even across the rooftops – she stood for a moment naked, arms extended towards the admiring moon; then, gathering her thin robe about her, descended into the darkness of her house.

For what seemed a long time I watched the spot from which she had departed as if the strength of my desire might bring her back. My resolution hardened. I thanked the Lord that he had granted me such a vision and I turned back into my chamber and rang a bell for a slave whom I sent to rouse my nephew Jonadab, whom I had made my chamberlain.

He came quickly rubbing sleep from his eyes, and yet the minutes that I waited seemed like hours. I described what I had seen and asked him straight out who the woman was.

Jonadab laughed. He was a slight, thin-faced, merry boy, a lover of gossip (which is why I had selected him for his position) and intrigue.

"It is extraordinary, my lord king," he said, "that you should have to inquire, for her name is Bathsheba and she is the most beautiful woman in Jerusalem."

"But who is she and why has she been kept from me?"

"My lord, she is very young, the granddaughter of Achitophel, and has only recently come to the city. Indeed it is only recently that she has become a beauty. Six months ago she was a plump and pretty girl, no more than that. I knew her as a child, and I must say I never thought . . ."

"Fetch her to me."

"But of course, my lord king, only" – he paused and gave me a smile in which I read mischief and perhaps some hesitation – "there is just one other thing you ought to know. She is no virgin but a married woman."

"A married woman? And Achitophel is her grandfather?"

"That is so. But . . ." Jonadab smiled again, and this time there was only mischief to be read – "her husband is not in Jerusalem. He is one Uriah, a Hittite, an officer in the bodyguard and at present serving the King at the siege of Rabbah. Does my uncle wish me to fetch her? Does the King wish me to fetch her?"

"Jonadab," I said, "I must have her. It is as simple and terrible as that. Whatever the consequences."

He smiled.

"I understand perfectly," he said. "But she is not a woman who can be summoned openly for what I understand so perfectly. Therefore I shall say to her that the King has received news concerning her husband by way of a messenger from the army, which he wishes to convey to her immediately and in person."

"Does she love her husband?"

"She married him at the command of her grandfather. Uriah has long been one of his agents."

"And will she come in response to such a summons?"

"Who can refuse the King?"

"And when you bring her to my bedchamber, what will she think?"

"Again, who can refuse the King?" He flashed a smile of delighted mockery. "What woman would wish to?"

To order what you should forbid: to do what you know you should not; is there a keener, more urgent delight? I rinsed my mouth with oil of peppermint to cleanse my breath. The hush of night was broken by barking of dogs in the gardens of the city. The stillness of the palace enfolded me. I pressed myself against the cool chaste marble of a column; music danced in every limb and organ. And I waited.

She came into my chamber with the light step of dawn, her robe disclosing a swelling breast, and her gaze damp and her soft lips parted.

"Rose of Sharon and lily of the valleys," I said.

She fell to her knees before me and took hold of my hands.

"You have word, my lord king, Jonadab tells me, of my husband Uriah."

I laid my hand in the soft forest of her hair and twined it in my fingers. I looked over her head at Jonadab, and made a sign that he should leave us. He retreated, smiling, and I drew up Bathsheba to her feet, and tilted her chin so that she might look into my eyes.

"You smell of almond blossom," I said. "I have no word of your husband."

"O my lord king, then I should not be here," she sighed, lowering her eyes but extending her lips towards me. I drew her to me and kissed her lips and fed upon roses and tasted delight. Her tongue searched out mine and danced. I slipped my hands under her thin robe and tore it apart and let it fall to the marble floor. I kissed her warm breasts and let my hands run over her body, and her flesh yielded and she pressed herself against me.

"I have loved the King," she murmured, "since I saw him when I was a little girl and had no breasts."

She leaned against my arms and I raised her up and carried her to the bed.

"O my dove, enter into the secret places . . . feed upon the lilies . . . until the day break . . . until the waters . . . the flowers appear on the earth . . . the voice of the turtle is heard . . . O my love, my dove . . ."

And so I entered into her and we were one flesh, three, no, four times, and she sighed the broken words of love, and then she slept in my arms, her deep dark-blue eyes closed in content, and the raven tresses of her hair spread over me. I tasted the wine of her body and my hand rested in the soft cleft, the secret place of delight between her thighs, and she moaned a little in her sleep and her hand that defied sleep clutched me. I eased my arm from under her and leaned over her and kissed the feathery smoothness of her belly, and she did not stir, but sighed gently in sweet surrender:

> You brought me almond blossom, and the breath
> Of a distant wind bearing sultry sweetness
> As of the sea was in your body.
> Joy of your clean-limbed flesh!
> Beyond love it is a ghost of that necessity
> Which breathes through the soul, so calm,
> And yet the desert wind carries it beyond the sunset.
> How small the world is, how light, in your hands!
> How the sands of the wilderness stretch empty beyond us.

Towards dawn she stirred, and there was neither anxiety nor – what I had feared – shame in her. She drew me to her again, and even then, as the light grew, was loth to depart.

"Set me as a seal upon your heart," she murmured, "for my love is strong as death . . ."

20 ∫

Was it because I knew from the first that Bathsheba would be the last woman to whom I should surrender my whole being, the last who would engage me utterly, that I made love to her with an intensity I had never known before? The loves of youth have their own ardour for they are voyages of exploration; but in the love of maturity, there is remembering too, and an awareness that the chariot of time is racing towards night's black embrace. Surrender I have said, but there was conquest also, for her inbreathing, gasping desire compelled her absolute submission to my demands. And then she knew, as if by nature, all the skills, refinements and devices by which pleasure is both intensified and prolonged – and indeed it must have been by nature, for she was adamant when I questioned her that her husband Uriah was unskilled in the art of love, and was accustomed as she said to mount her with the brutal thrust of a bull, caring nothing for her pleasure. Pleasure indeed! – a weak and half-dead word to describe what we experienced together! She had the ardour of my wild, half-tamed Maacah, coupled with an imagination and dexterity which I had only before known in a Philistine courtesan.

One morning, wakening in her arms, and sensing the eager passion of the still sleeping flesh pressed against me, I thought of how Michal had ever kept a part, perhaps the essential part, of herself from me, denying me that worshipful submission which, compelling the lover's own surrender, makes male and female one flesh, one being, each at the same moment conqueror and conquered.

And at that moment I wondered how I could ever have supposed I truly loved Michal; true love bespeaks perfect knowledge, and she forbade me that.

Bathsheba awoke then with a strange, for a moment distant, and even dangerous look in her glistening eye; then that look fled, as if it had been intended for another who might share her bed, but one from whom she would receive no satisfaction, with whom she would never know rapture, but whose advances she would receive as a duty, with indifference. And then she smiled, that half-smile at the corner of her mouth and in her eyes, a smile that was welcoming, lascivious in its sensual and voluptuous certainty, a smile that drew me to her, and into her, annihilating distinction of sex and being, while yet at the same time enhancing my sense of both. She took what I offered, what I did, to her and with her, as if all the acts which we created together were one act, an enduring celebration of the union of man and woman, body and soul, time past and time present.

We made love as day returned to the city and the sun lit up our bed with its rays of life.

There was danger in her too-frequent visits to the palace, for the Law of Moses is harsh, and the penalty for adultery death.

When she thought of Uriah she wept, but with anger, not pity; and she cursed Achitophel who had forced that marriage on her, and so made her love a sin against the Law; for we both knew that even the King may not transgress the Law, and that, against the Law, if Uriah chose to summon it to his aid, not even my protection could secure her life. She recognised this, being as intelligent as she was beautiful, and knowing that the priests hold power even over kings. And the consciousness of our sin and her danger was like a thundercloud rising behind forbidding mountains in the bright morning of our love.

So I formed the habit of slipping from the palace when night fell and making my way, disguised, to Bathsheba's house. Her old nurse, of whose fidelity she was confident, was the only person we admitted to the secret, and she was at least discreet enough to respect my anonymity and give me no hint that she recognised the King, though naturally I knew that my disguise did not deceive her.

Bathsheba loved to hear me tell of my exploits, of the wars and battles in which I had been engaged, of the wrath of Saul, and the love of Jonathan. To her alone, I confessed my antipathy to Joab and she responded by warning me against her grandfather, Achitophel.

"Believe me, my love, he is corrupted by jealousy. Though you have made him a great man in Israel, he believes he should be greater still, and because he is secretive and deceitful by nature, your virtue rebukes him. He forced my marriage on me to bind Uriah to him, and Uriah reports to him everything that comes to pass in the army, every rumour that he hears, every disaffection that is expressed; and Achitophel uses Uriah in order to attract young officers to himself, so that they come to believe that they owe loyalty to him rather than to you, the King."

One night she wept and when I pressed her, said: "I am afraid. Uriah is a fierce and violent man. When he discovers our love, our love . . ." and her voice tailed off.

"But do you think I shall not protect you?"

"Against the Law?"

"Against the Law."

But I knew she did not believe me, or trust my power. I took her in my arms to prove again the force of my love, and for a time she lay there, trembling as if she would deny herself to me. Then as I explored her body the trembling ceased, and she gave herself to me with an abandonment so complete that I knew the depths of her fear and apprehension.

"Uriah has never used me as a woman should be used," she murmured. "I never knew delight till . . . again, again, take me to the mountain of myrrh, to the hill of frankincense, O my beloved, put thy hand in the hole of the door, and I will open to you . . ."

"My love, Bathsheba, my secret garden of delights . . . how much better is thy love than wine and the smell of thy body than all spices . . ."

(Why, now, do I torture myself with these memories, writing thoughts as broken words, the broken words of songs, of the music of the heavens that is never played by earthly instrument?

Thinking of Bathsheba I transform her into Michal, who never made me free in this manner of her being, and I summon Abishag to bring me relief with her cherry lips, to draw from me my distress, that I may find delight through knowing her ashamed obedience . . .)

And then she told me that she was with child.

In her mingled joy and terror her beauty trembled in my eyes. The temples of her head were touched with dew, and her lips quivered like leaves in the wind of her fear.

"Uriah will force a trial upon me," she sobbed, "and the King cannot confess his sin before all the people."

Then she said: "My nurse Sarah will remove the child from me."

I did not understand at first. I thought: that will not serve for she will not be able to disguise her condition from the world, nor conceal the knowledge from Uriah or Achitophel. I feared – yes, feared – that Achitophel would find in my love the means to destroy me.

And then I knew what she intended, and cried out:

"No. The child's life is the Lord's gift."

I said to her the next day:

"I shall summon Uriah from the army. I shall find some pretext that none will suspect. And then I shall send him to you, and you must let him lie with you. So he will believe the child to be his, and all will be well."

She looked at me with reproach.

"If you loved me, you would not ask me to lie with another man."

"He is your husband."

"I mean," she said, "especially with my husband. If you loved me, you would not ask me to lie with my husband who has never been a true husband to me."

"It is because I love you and care for you that I ask you to do this."

For a long time she resisted, hating reality, as women do.

"If you loved me," she said, "you would abandon all for my

sake, you would resign the throne to Amnon, and carry me off with you. I would live content with you in the wilderness."

I knew she lied. I knew she did not know she was lying, but deceived herself.

"Do not be angry with me, my beloved," she said, "because I am weak and fearful, but I cannot do as you ask. I cannot submit myself to that man. I would rather die."

I pressed her head against me and put my tongue to her ear and spoke sweet words of love, and she cried out:

"I am sick of love. Love has made me, love unmakes me. Why, my beloved, did you behold me on the rooftops, why did you come to me like a young hart, to make me dance upon the mountains in a dance that will destroy me? I was not alive till you touched me."

I cajoled, I persuaded, I reasoned; all in vain. Then I took her and she moaned, "Let me die, O Lord, in love," and I licked salt tears from her cheeks.

But in the dawn, she repaired her face; she confronted the rising sun, and said it should be as I wished.

"But I do it," she said, "for your sake, that you may not be disgraced before all the people, for I would myself choose death."

She drew me to her, demanding love as if there should be no tomorrow, as if we lay in a garden which encompassed the whole world.

21

He stood before me, a black brute of a man, and smirked. He moved his heavy body awkwardly. I questioned him about the siege of Rabbah and about the state of mind of the troops. I hinted that Achitophel had let me know that he, Uriah, was a man I could rely on to report any disaffection, any doubts as to the manner in which Joab was conducting the investment of the city. I sought his opinion as to why it was taking so long. I let him understand that I was worried, that Joab sent me reports which I found disquieting but yet had no solid reason to doubt. I said, in almost so many words, that the power of the King was limited, since he had to rely on information given him by those in whom he had of necessity put his trust, but who might find reason to deceive him. That was why I had summoned him to me, because Achitophel had assured me that he was a man in whom I might repose infinite confidence. Furthermore, I said, I understood that Achitophel had demonstrated his own trust in him, and high regard for him, by giving him his granddaughter in marriage, a girl, I had been informed, of remarkable beauty and virtue, worthy of a great warrior. I may even have gone so far – indeed I did go so far – as to imply that on the recommendation of Achitophel I had marked out Uriah for promotion, even to the highest level; Joab, after all, was ageing and his powers might be in decline.

He answered me in that bluff, bullying, soldierly manner which I have always despised, and with that peculiar thoughtless self-confidence which derives from an utter insensitivity to others. As he spoke, Bathsheba's view of him was confirmed:

the man was surly, heavy, and self-righteous, without a spark of imagination. He would certainly be jealous.

At the same time it was evident – for I wish to be fair to him, all the more so because he awoke in me a sense of revulsion for his person – that he evinced a certain grasp of purely military affairs. His comments on the conduct of the siege did not lack sense. When, provoked to rashness by the sympathy I displayed, he spoke slightingly of Joab's conduct of affairs, I recognised shrewdness in his judgement. I couldn't deny that he was probably an efficient regimental officer, though his innate brutality displayed in the manner of speech and indeed in the very way in which he shifted that heavy ox-like body suggested that he would command the fear, rather than the affection, of the soldiers under him. When to impress me he told me how he had quelled an incipient outbreak of mutiny, my admiration of his efficiency (assuming he reported truthfully) was tempered by the disgust which his clear relish in the punishment he had inflicted aroused in me.

Nevertheless I praised him, even flattered him, for it was my intention to make him believe that he had found favour in my sight; and, besides, nothing gives a man so good an opinion of a superior as the bestowal of praise by him.

"I see you are a soldier of rare calibre," I said, "a man after my own heart, and one on whose good sense and perspicacity I can rely."

Then I examined him closely, in great detail, about the fortifications of Rabbah, and in doing so took care to remind him, without his being aware that I was doing so, that I was myself a general of great experience and renown, to whom he was fortunate to be talking as an equal.

Finally I said: "I am more grateful to you, Uriah, than I can say. You can have little idea how difficult it is for me here, of necessity removed from the battle, to obtain a clear and coherent picture of how things are at the front. You have most admirably filled in the gaps inevitably left in the other reports I have received, and you have suggested measures to which I shall give much thought, and which I am certain should, many of them at least, be put into effect. Achitophel, on whose wise advice I have long relied, as I am sure you are aware, spoke very highly of you to me. I expected therefore to be impressed, knowing that he is not a man given to exaggeration, but I am even more impressed than I had thought to be. I am therefore very grateful to you for the time you have given me, for your clear exposition of the state of things, to which you have evidently devoted much intelligent consideration. But you are a young man, and no doubt a lusty one, and I have kept you longer than is reasonable from the delights which a soldier expects on leave. You will be eager to be with your wife, and, if she is as beautiful as report has it, understandably eager. So I shall now release you to her loving arms, and I have no doubt you will acquit yourself as nobly in the bed as in the field of battle. And to show my approbation of your conduct, and also to compensate your lady, whose name, I am ashamed to say, I do not recall – such, my friend, are the ravages of age, or rather the penalty of growing old – I shall have a dish of rare and fine food sent from my kitchens to your house, if you will give me your direction, and also wine of the finest vintage, and in this way I shall hope to appease her, so that she may forgive me for the unconscionable time I have kept you from her. And so you may take your leave of me, with my thanks and my heartfelt wish that you may enjoy a night of love, you young dog, as you deserve to do."

My last words may have been double-edged, but I did not think he would notice that. Indeed, ignorant as he was, there was no reason why he should. He withdrew, and, as he turned after retreating twenty paces backwards, and marched away from me, he kicked his legs out in that conceited, self-satisfied, and ill-bred manner which I have always detested, seeing in it a physical arrogance that reflects a brutish soul.

Nevertheless I was well pleased with our talk. On the one hand, the dislike he had aroused in me freed me from any feelings of guilt I might have had at the thought that I had made him a cuckold – indeed he aroused such repugnance in me that even if I had not already lain (many times) with his wife, I might have wished to do so now. On the other hand I had done what I had set out to do. I do not think I could have made it clearer without expressly ordering him to – no, even now I shrink from the word in this connection, just as at the time the thought of him making the beast with two backs with Bathsheba – my adored and lovely Bathsheba – made me sick to the stomach and churned my bowels.

Well, I told myself, I could take my revenge when he had done that which he had to do.

Then even that thought turned on me, for I saw that, though I longed to humiliate him and reduce him to a grovelling heap begging for mercy to me, I could not do so without abandoning Bathsheba – which was unthinkable.

I could not sleep that night, and soon after dawn called Jonadab to my chamber. He arrived rubbing his eyes.

"Send at once," I said, "to his house, and summon Uriah the Hittite to me. I must speak with him again before he returns to the army."

"There will be no need for such a summons," he said, "for I stumbled over him as I made my way through the guard-room. He didn't wake, though I kicked his head. I doubt if he will be fit to travel early. He will have a head like a sore bear."

"Are you telling me," I said, "he did not lie with his wife last night?"

I thought: she was not his, perhaps she drove him away, unable to overcome the revulsion with which the prospect of his embraces filled her. Then I thought: but, if so, she has destroyed herself.

Jonadab knew of my affair with Bathsheba. He did not know she was with child. Therefore, when he told me that Uriah lay drunk in the guard-room, he believed that he was bringing me news I would wish to hear. And, since he thought that was so, he might be lying. But I did not dare to send to Bathsheba to inquire.

Jonadab said: "When he left you, it may have been his intention to go to his wife, but he fell in with old comrades among the officers of the guard. They began drinking, and Uriah boasting of his exploits before Rabbah. One thing led to another, and when I retired Uriah was well advanced in insensibility. And so the fool lies drunk. That is all."

He smiled with happy malice, confident that he pleased me.

Perhaps, with that end in mind, he himself had tempted Uriah to drink deep. For a moment I thought of admitting him to my full confidence; but the secret being not mine but my love's, did not do so. Instead I dismissed him, and remained a long while in perplexity, seeing no one but my chamber-boy. Before Jonadab left, however, I charged him with the duty of cancelling my engagements for that morning.

"You were to give an audience to Achitophel," he said.

"Tell him I cannot. Tell him I am out of sorts. But do it gently and without emphasis, so that he is not offended and not curious."

I thought of Bathsheba, happy that her husband had not come to her, terrified on account of the consequences of his failure to do so. She had steeled herself to receive him, and now I pictured her bright courage darkening as fear invaded her like a wind from the desert.

In the afternoon I summoned Uriah to me again. He came before me, his breath stinking from his debauch. I laughed as a veteran might laugh to another, simulating fellow feeling, and called for wine. I pressed a goblet on him, and drank myself, and looking over the rim of my glass, said,

"What a backward fellow you are that seem so loath to pleasure yourself with a lady reported beautiful by all!"

And I clapped him on the back, and poured more wine.

"My lord king," he said, "I am a plain soldier and blunt of speech."

He paused, and I knew a moment's apprehension, for he spoke like a man who has discovered his wife's infidelity, and I wondered what rumours he might have heard from his fellow officers. Though I had taken all possible precautions to keep my affair with Bathsheba secret, and to shield her from the disclosure of what the priests and the world would call her shame, yet in such matters, there is near always something known, some suspicion raised, and I could not be certain that Uriah was still ignorant of his disgrace. For one thing, I had no doubt that Achitophel paid agents in my own household to report my comings and goings to him. In my black mood I was all at once certain we had been betrayed.

But I smiled: "Even a blunt soldier pines for women. Even the noblest man of war must satisfy other desires."

"My lord king," he said, "the Ark of the Lord, and Israel and Judah abide in tents, and I have come from the army where my lord Joab and the servants of my lord are camped in the barren plain. Why then should I go to my house, to sleep in sheets and take delight in a woman? The thought disgusts me, and I will not do it."

The stupidity and complacency of the speech so angered me that I had difficulty in restraining myself from either striking him or putting him under arrest – to teach him sense and better manners. Had not I, the King, urged him to attend to his wife, and had he not disobeyed me?

But, again, I smiled, and threw off a joke about the soldier's duty extending to the breeding of warriors.

"But I see," I said, "that you are a man of firm principle. We shall dine together this evening and then I shall take the opportunity to persuade you that one duty – the duty you owe your king – does not exclude another, which you owe your wife; but that indeed the two commingle in the duty you owe to Israel."

Throughout the day I longed to send to Bathsheba so that I might know how she was; and yet I dared not. It occurred to me in the afternoon that Uriah might have gone to her then, and I inquired of Jonadab where he was.

"Playing dice with your officers and boasting of the favour in which he stands with you, my lord king."

I fed him wine at dinner and talked bawdy, speaking of my delight in women, and telling tales of love, in the hope that this would stir his lust, and he would go to his wife. But though Uriah laughed, and retorted with stories of his own, in which there was neither wit nor beauty, but in which I rather read a hatred for women and relish in humiliating them, that made me sick to the stomach when I thought of this brute thrusting at my love, he showed no eagerness to be with her.

Yet, when he staggered drunkenly from my presence, I could not be certain that he would not go to her; and hatred possessed my soul.

In the dark of night I turned dark thoughts in my mind, and when the cocks crowed as the first touch of dawn lit the sky, I knew I could not be content, while Uriah shared the earth with me.

I said to myself: he boasts of being a soldier . . . well, let him die a soldier's death.

In the morning I called Uriah to me again, and ordered him to return to the army. I entrusted him with a message to carry to Joab. He received it with pride, ignorant that he carried his own death warrant.

22

Of course I did not order Joab to have Uriah killed. There was no need for that. I could rely on Joab to read between the lines; it was the sort of task he relished. So I was able to console Bathsheba with the assurance that all would be well. I expressed my relief that her husband should not have stirred himself to visit her, and, if she felt his failure to do so to be a doubtful testimony to her charms, I was soon able by my ardour to convince her that it was merely evidence of Uriah's ill taste. For the moment then she was happy to let the future take care of itself, to trust that I would see her right, and to gather the roses of love while they were yet fresh.

Three days later – I think it was three days, but it may well have been four – yes, perhaps it was four – a messenger came to me from Joab in the camp at Rabbah. He was a young man, whom I did not recognise, and he was begrimed and appeared nervous. He fell on his knees before me.

"My lord king, great in battle, I come from the lord Joab, your Highness's most faithful and, he bids me say, today his most unhappy servant. For Rabbah, which we besieged, is still in the hands of the enemy, and a great assault against the walls of the city has failed."

Then, with lowered head, he described to me how Joab had launched a frontal attack at a part of the city wall which he believed to be but feebly manned, at least in comparison with other stretches. But either he had been deceived or spies had discovered his intention, for the attack was repulsed with – he heaved a sob – great loss of life.

I questioned him keenly, for it seemed to me that in exposing so large a part of his force to such a dubious enterprise Joab had acted with unforgivable rashness, had taken a gamble which was unnecessary, since he had only to maintain his blockade of the city to ensure its eventual capture. I bit back the suggestion that Joab's capacities were failing, his judgement gone awry, for it would not have been suitable to express such doubts to a mere messenger.

Then, as if sensing my gathering anger, the young man lifted his head, and said:

"My lord Joab also told me to inform you that to his great regret your servant Uriah the Hittite is among the dead."

I turned away, and touched my eye with a cloth as if to staunch my tears. I looked over the city. The air was very still, and there was silence in the heat of the afternoon sun, which made the leaves of the olive trees across the valley glisten and shimmer. I looked to the roof of Bathsheba's dwelling, and thought how she had waited there trembling for fear that she would hear Uriah's footsteps. A great peace descended on me, and my heart sang towards the Lord.

The young man now recited a catalogue of the dead in battle, and when I heard the name of Laish among them, I did weep.

"For the dark places of the earth are filled with the habitations of cruelty," I murmured, and remembered how he had come to me trusting and eager in love; and now his flesh was food for the birds of death. But when the messenger concluded with the repetition of the name of Uriah, I dried my eyes, and called for wine to refresh the young man, and said to him:

"Tell my lord Joab not to be downhearted and not to grieve, for this is the fortune of war, and the sword devours one man as well as another. So urge him, or say I urge him, to renew the battle against the city and overthrow it, that our dead may not have fallen in vain. And say to him that, now as ever, he has found favour in my sight, for I know there is no man braver in Israel, and none in whom I rest more absolute trust."

Then I called Jonadab, and ordered him to send to inform Bathsheba of her husband's death, gallant in battle, to convey my condolences to her, and to bid her to put on mourning for a man who had died serving Israel and his king.

And I did this, so that none might point the finger at her.

When I came to her, secretly, that night, we did not speak of Uriah, who was to us both now as chaff blown by the wind.

She was still in mourning when it became apparent that she was with child, and men said how sad it was that Uriah should have been taken from her before his son was born. Only, Bathsheba told me, her grandfather Achitophel looked at her curiously, and made as if to speak – "It was in my mind to reproach me," she said – but then held his peace.

"When we are married," she said, "I would wish that you dismiss him from his post, and banish him from Israel. Or at least from Jerusalem. It disturbs me to see him, for I believe he suspects."

"Suspects? What is there to suspect? That the child is mine? When we are married, who will care who the child's father may be?"

"I think he suspects more than that."

I took her in my arms.

"What is there to suspect more than that? Uriah came here, I used him with honour. I urged him to go to you. Who dares to swear that he did not do so, that he disobeyed the King's command? Not even Achitophel. And then Uriah died bravely in battle, a soldier's death – a battle in which my close, much-loved, and most faithful friend, Laish, also fell. I was seen by the messenger who brought me word of their deaths, to shed tears. Besides, my love, Achitophel should be proud and happy to see you queen."

"Nevertheless," she said, "I fear him."

Bathsheba judged more wisely than I. That may seem strange, for she was but a young girl, ignorant of the ways of the world. How Achitophel came to believe that I was responsible for Uriah's death, I do not know; but I am certain that the rumours of, at least, my complicity, which Jonadab brought to me, originated from that counsellor whom I had once honoured with my trust, but who now sought to destroy me.

"Do men accuse me of murder?" I asked Jonadab.

"Not precisely, my lord king, but they say that Uriah's death fell very happily for you; and there are some who mutter, I am told, that Joab ordered that men should fall away from Uriah in the battle."

"This is foolishness. Do they not know that Laish was also killed, and do they suppose that 'fell happily' for me?"

But Jonadab looked away and would not answer that question; and it was as if I heard Achitophel's thin voice insinuating that David would sacrifice even his dearest friend to destroy Uriah, whose wife he coveted.

There would be many, such is the baseness of man, to believe him.

I ordered Jonadab to set spies about Achitophel. He was clearly spreading disaffection, and there were some, especially among the young men, ready to listen to him. They were those who had grown up while I was king, who knew no other and who were restless and eager for a change. But though I was certain that Achitophel was fomenting discontent, I could obtain no evidence. So I kept him about me, and in his office, thinking that he might be more dangerous still if I dismissed him, and made his grievance, and my distrust, manifest.

And I also wondered if Joab had spoken rashly, perhaps in his cups, as he sometimes did; and I held this suspicion against him also.

A few weeks after I had married Bathsheba, and the birth of our son, Nathan the prophet, a man whom I esteemed, came to me.

"Blessed be the Lord God of Israel," he said, and sat on the earth before me, and pulled his beard.

"David," he said, "you know, my lord king, that I have ever loved you and served you with all my heart, under the Lord."

"I know," I replied, not liking something I read in his manner.

"Let me tell you a story," he said. "There were two men in a certain city. One of them was exceeding rich and the other equally poor. The rich man had many flocks and herds, but the poor man had nothing except one little ewe lamb, which he had reared and tended with great care and love, as if it had been his daughter or even his wife. Now a traveller came to the rich man, and he set himself to feed him. But rather than take a lamb from his own flock" – Nathan paused and raised his head and looked me in the eye, and his gaze was dark and melancholy and seemed full of pain – "rather than do that, he took hold of the poor man's lamb, to provide a feast for his guest."

He looked at me inquiringly. I was disquieted by his story, and spoke almost without reflection.

"If there is any justice," I said, "Your rich man should be punished. And, as I am a judge in Israel, so he shall be. Tell me who he is, and I will have him brought before me."

Nathan shook his head.

"There is no need for that, David. You are that rich man."

Then he stood up, while I was silent, and said:

"This is the word of the Lord of Hosts, the Lord God of Israel: I anointed thee King over Israel, by the hand of Samuel my prophet, and when Saul rose against thee, I saved thee from his anger. And I made thee king and gave thee wives and great riches. But thou hast turned against me, and done evil in my sight, disdaining my commandment; and hast killed Uriah the Hittite, basely, and taken his wife, basely. Therefore the sword shall never depart from thy house, because thou hast despised me and taken the wife of Uriah the Hittite. Hear the word of the Lord, O King; I shall raise up evil against thy house, and I shall take thy wives from thee, and give them to thy neighbour that he may lie with them openly in the sight of the world. For, David, thou didst this secretly, but the Lord shall act openly, that all the world may see your transgression and know that not even the King is above the Law of the Lord of Hosts."

He spoke in that archaic language which the priests and prophets employ to make their speech more impressive; as with Samuel, I found myself wondering to what extent the words were indeed the Lord's and to what extent His prophet's. Yet they disturbed me. When Samuel spoke out against Saul and denounced him in the name of the Lord, no candid listener could avoid the thought that the divine anger chimed uncommonly well with Samuel's own jealousy of Saul who had supplanted him in the government of Israel. But Nathan had ever been my supporter. He claimed only moral authority, and I knew that he both loved and admired me.

I said: "Nathan, what do you charge me with?"

"You have heard what I have spoken," he said.

"The tongue is the tongue of Nathan, but the words sound to me as if they were spoken by Achitophel."

"The words are the Lord's, my king."

He looked sorrowfully on me, and as he did so I felt diminished, for I knew he spoke the truth. I did not regret Uriah's death, but I wished I had slain him more fittingly, with my own hand. The manner in which I had compassed his death was mean, I could not deny that. And yet it was impossible that I should have done it any other way, without laying Bathsheba open to insult, and, indeed, worse.

I said: "Nathan, Bathsheba is ignorant of what I have done, therefore innocent. But you are right."

I turned away from him, and, gazing towards the hills, felt myself a prisoner of my palace, my achievement, and my love.

"I have sinned against the Lord," I said, "and done evil in His sight."

I fell to my knees and cried out:

"Lord, I acknowledge my transgressions. My sin is even before me. Against thee, O Lord, have I sinned, and all the sacrifice I bring to Thee is a troubled spirit, a broken and a contrite heart, which I pray that Thou wilt not despise."

While I prayed in this manner, Nathan touched me, gently, on the head, and, having rested his hand there a little while, took his leave and left me to the anxious dark and to my shame and the fear of the Lord.

But I said nothing of this to Bathsheba.

For a time I believed that the Lord had forgiven me, and I banished the memory of Uriah.

When Joab returned victorious from the siege of Rabbah, and reported that the city was taken and a great number of the enemy slain, I embraced him before all the people, and held a feast in his honour; but not even in his cups was there any talk of Uriah. Yet I felt uncomfortable with Joab, as if for the first time he had an advantage over me.

A little later the son born to Bathsheba fell sick. His fever was high. Bathsheba sat by his cot, watching over his agony. I turned to the Lord and abased myself before Him, calling Him to witness that I repented my sin, and urging Him to spare my child. For seven days I neither ate nor drank but wrestled with the Lord in an attempt to save the little boy.

But my sin was too great. The Lord would not be moved to mercy. The child died, and as she stood before me, with the small body in her arms, Bathsheba knew what she had refused to know before: the price at which I had bought her life and our love.

She said: "I had rather have been stoned to death for adultery than that this should happen."

She turned away, and denied herself to me.

Well, that was how it was; the clouds and a cold wind lay over our love. I had sinned for Bathsheba's sake and was punished for her sin, and for a long time she would not listen to me, but denied me. We came together again. We made another child, whom we called Solomon – the young prig who now waits for my death. But it was never the same again. There was an emptiness in our love, because Bathsheba could not forgive me for what I had done for her. She knew she was wrong not to forgive me; and yet she could not. The shadow of the dead child lay even on our bed.

Book III ∫

23

I have seen all the works that are done under the sun; and all is vanity and vexation of spirit. Soon after Solomon was born I entered into the fall of years. I had achieved everything, and the fruit was bitter. The kings from all the lands that bordered on Israel did me honour and acknowledged my virtue, my power, and my wisdom; and I cared less for their words than for the praise which the girls gathered around the well in my youth had lavished on my songs.

I said to myself: to everything there is a season, and a time to every purpose under heaven.

When I was young – I thought – in the glory of the morning, I acted on the world; now the world acts on me, and shadows creep gigantic on the sands of life.

I found in my perplexity little pleasure in women or in the search for wisdom; nor in strong drink nor dancing. Bathsheba no longer delighted me, but I sought no pleasure in her stead. Often I conversed with Nathan, because he knew my heart; but he could not restore it to blitheness.

I hung the trumpet of war in my house, and left battles and the quest for glory to others. There were days when I longed for death, and nights when I feared its coming. The music that I made was melancholy, and my songs were full of bitterness.

A wise man, grown old, seeks delight in his children, but mine brought me only trouble.

Towards Amnon I felt protective, my firstborn, conceived and brought forth in the midst of dangers. He was my heir, who should rule the empire of Israel. Achitophel had tried to set me against him; in vain. I loved him for his very frailty.

Amnon was not easy in conversation. He was dark and secretive. He could not trust in himself or inspire trust in others. As he grew up he consorted with wild youths a few years older than himself, who were pleased to know the King's son, to lead him astray, to teach him to drink deep and to despise women. Amnon then learned to affect a rough, soldierly manner, and I read in it a profound desire to be other than he was. In Amnon I saw a resemblance to Saul, though there was no blood connection. Curiously the one woman with whom he found himself at ease was Michal, who now resided in a house a few miles beyond Jerusalem. There, it was told to me, Amnon spent many hours in conversation with her. He would go to her when he was troubled. Perhaps she saw in him a reflection of that discontent which she had always known herself, that inability ever to forget or lose awareness of the picture which she at each moment presented. Like Michal, Amnon could not lose himself in action; it was as if he observed everything that he did; and even in action, scorned what he did and found it worthless.

I said to myself: Amnon hates himself. Is it my fault that he is like this?

How different were the children of Maacah, my wild Arab girl from the northern desert. Absalom, my son, was the most beautiful youth in Israel, Tamar, my daughter, the loveliest girl. They were as reflections of each other, for both seemed to possess the charms of both sexes. To see either move was to be witness to a celebration of life.

I knew Amnon to be jealous of Absalom. He accused me of preferring his younger brother. What could I say? I could not tell him the truth: that I adored Absalom for his perfections, and loved Amnon for his imperfections. So I fobbed him off with some answer so vague as to seem insincere. But I assured him, yet again, that he was my heir, and that he should be king after me.

Did I send him away thinking that I loved him only from duty, but Absalom by nature?

* * *

I do not know, only that I was blind, occupied with my own thoughts and my increasing distress.

One day, Jonadab came to me, with his insidious smile and wriggling his hindquarters like a bitch on heat. I trusted him, because I had few to trust.

He said: "My lord king, Amnon is sick. Will you come visit him?"

So I did, and found him lying on his bed in his chamber, very pale and weak, as if he had not eaten but suffered a fever. When he spoke it was in a low voice so that I had to lean over him, and he took my hand and pressed it.

I said: "I shall send Bathsheba to you, for she understands sickness better than I do."

He whispered: "Do not trouble the Queen, but beg my sister Tamar to come to me. I have no appetite and yet I feel a strong desire to eat those little almond cakes she makes."

A strange request, but Amnon looked so pale, weak, and unhappy that I could not refuse him. There was no question of refusing him.

I have never known just what happened subsequently, for different versions of the story were told me.

I became aware of a shrinking and a silence in the palace. There was an atmosphere of acute anxiety, as if some calamity had occurred, and none dared to tell the King. Yet Israel was at peace. I sent for Jonadab to inquire. He would not look me in the face and protested that he knew nothing.

"Is Amnon dead?" I asked. "Is my son dead?"

"No, my lord king, Amnon lives."

I said: "It is clear to me that you are concealing something fearful. Tell me what it is, and do not fear my anger for I know you are innocent of any wrongdoing."

"Oh, my lord king," he said, "I wish I were."

Then he fell to the ground and clutched me by the knees and wept.

"Jonadab," I said, "you are my sister's son, close to me in blood, and dear on account of the service you have done me. You need not fear my anger."

"My lord king, be merciful. Amnon your son is sick, but his

sickness is of the mind and not the body. He is sick with love for his sister – his half-sister – Tamar . . ."

At that moment, without ceremony, the door was thrown open and Absalom entered unannounced. He paused when he saw Jonadab with his arms still round my legs. I raised Jonadab up, and turned to Absalom. There was no colour in his cheeks, though his eye was star-bright.

"Father," he cried . . . but I cannot write down the words that he spoke. His speech was full of oaths, and he was half mad with grief and fury.

He told me that Tamar had gone as I had arranged to visit Amnon, and then he had dismissed his attendants, and, alone with the girl, declared his love. "His love," Absalom spat the words. "Say rather his lust, his perverted lust."

"And what did she say?"

"She said . . . she said . . . she said she was sorry for him."

I did not want to hear more. Absalom forced me to listen. He told me how Amnon had then seized Tamar, torn her gown and thrown her on the bed, and raped her.

"And this thing with you now," Absalom cried, "was his pimp, his pander."

Jonadab whimpered a half-denial. I silenced him with a look.

After the awful deed, Absalom said, Amnon had turned from Tamar, as if with disgust, as if he were the victim, and ordered her to go. Absalom himself had found her, throwing dust on her head, and howling her despair, in the public street. He had taken her to his house, and come straight to me.

"I did not know that was Amnon's intention," Jonadab said. "Please believe me, I did not know."

"She is defiled," Absalom cried – and his voice was like the howl of a wolf in the desert. Though he was pale as death, sweat stood out on his brow. "I know the Law," he said.

"The Law. This is no matter for the Law."

"The Law." Absalom's voice was now quiet and he spoke with authority. "If a man shall take his sister, his father's daughter, and see her nakedness, and she see his nakedness, it is a wicked thing; and they shall be cut off in the sight of the people; he hath uncovered his sister's nakedness; he shall bear his iniquity. That is the Law. And Amnon, who was my brother, has done worse than that, for he has taken Tamar by force, without her consent, and raped her."

At that moment I knew, sharply, the agony of Saul, for it seemed that the Lord had deserted me.

Amnon was my child, my firstborn, and I was responsible for him, blood of my blood, flesh of my flesh. If he was guilty, I could not hold myself innocent. The ghost of Uriah was knocking at my door.

Jonadab said: "He only asked me for advice as to how he could plead his love. I never imagined . . ."

Poor Amnon, I thought, but dared not say, to be driven by despair to such extremity. And again I thought of Saul.

I said whatever might be said to comfort and appease Absalom.

Then I said: "First, we must ensure Tamar's protection. She has been violated and rejected, a double shame, which for her sake must be concealed."

"Concealed? For her sake?"

"Absalom, my son, my darling, would you drive her mad? You talk in your anger, your righteous anger, of the Law. Do you think you know the Law as well as I do? Would you expose the poor girl to its rigour, its severity? Would you have her compelled publicly to confess her shame? Never."

So I worked on him, and what I said was true and of great weight, and he understood me. I swore him to silence, "for the time being," I said.

"We have enemies," I said, "even in Israel who would feed greedily on this crime."

I praised his ardour. I commended the love for his sister which fired it. But I insisted on silence. I said I must consult Bathsheba, who was wise in such matters. It crossed my mind that perhaps Amnon should marry Tamar – I was sure it could be arranged – she was only his half-sister – but I did not speak of this to Absalom. I told him to bring Tamar to me when she was well enough and ready to see me; meanwhile to guard her well and offer her such comfort as he could. I took him in my arms and kissed him, and held him to me, and drank of his youth and strength.

"He has destroyed her," he said. "The rose of Israel is torn and its petals scattered."

"Absalom, my son, my dearest son, go in peace, and the Lord be with you this terrible day."

When he departed, I ordered Jonadab speedily to put a guard over Amnon.

"Take his weapons from him," I said, "lest in his despair he kill himself."

"Am I to put him under arrest?"

"No," I said, "place the guard cunningly. It is there for his protection, no more than that. But go yourself, also, and say to him that it is my wish that he keep his house till I come to him. This is a business that will require fine management, if it is not to destroy us all, to destroy the house of David."

24

Tamar did not recover. She was more beautiful than ever, but her beauty was altered. It was the beauty of winter now; the leaves were stripped from her tree of life, and her roses cast on the wild wind. She had the beauty of all good things that we know to have lost. Her eyes wandered and her cheeks were white as mountain snow. She took no care of her dress, or of her modesty; shame now lodged in her heart, and, broken by the world and the flesh, she would force the world to confess its cruelty. She babbled strangely. One day she was found soliciting in the street, her mind unhinged, and, from that hour, I was compelled to order that she be confined.

Absalom alone commanded her trust. When I spoke to her she whimpered, and either hid her face behind her veil, or, more terribly, exposed herself to me, as if being Amnon's father I was also her seducer, whom in that mood she was determined to confront with the enormity of his action. But she clung to Absalom as a little child may cling to those whom she trusts. I feared that her helplessness and her woe would kindle the fires of his anger with Amnon into a renewed blaze, and I was tempted to forbid him to be with his sister. But I did not dare to yield to this temptation, for fear of his refusal and the consequences of such a refusal.

I was able however to persuade Absalom to make his peace with Amnon, when I released his brother from the secret house arrest under which I had in effect placed him. They embraced before me, and Amnon, coached by myself and Hushai, who pitied him as I did, confessed his sin, and sought his brother's forgiveness.

"For our father's sake," Absalom replied.

It had proved impossible to keep what had happened secret as I would have wished.

Joab came to me, and said: "David, even the army is divided. Some support Amnon, others Absalom. If you do not resolve the matter, things will get worse. The open wound will fester. If Amnon is to be king, then Absalom must be sent into exile, for the kingdom cannot contain the pair of them."

Bathsheba agreed with him. She had a tenderness for Amnon – or so it seemed to me then. She understood his difficult character.

"Yes," she said, "Amnon has done wrong. What he did was wicked. But he was provoked. You adore Absalom and are blind to his faults. You may not even know how Absalom encouraged the young men whom he attracts about him to mock his brother, how he spread rumours – or at least fanned rumours – that Amnon was perverted; how at the same time he encouraged Tamar to flaunt her charms before him."

I found it hard to believe her, because – of course – I did not wish to do so. And I knew she was jealous of Absalom. Perhaps even then, I think now, even then, though Solomon was only a little boy, she was determined that he should be king after me; and saw Absalom, not my poor Amnon, as his chief rival. I did not know if she spoke the truth, though these suspicions have come upon me in the gathering dark of years.

Achitophel also approached me. Though I had learned to distrust him, I still felt the charm of his manner and his intellect.

"David," he said, "we have lived through much together, not always agreeing one with the other, but nevertheless both working for the good of Israel. And you know that I have always spoken my mind, fearlessly and not hiding from the truth. It is natural that you should do that now, for Amnon is your son, and you love him as you love his brother Absalom. Believe me, old friend, I feel for you in your dilemma. But I remember also the boy who came to Saul's camp and went against Goliath when all the army were afraid of him, and how you slew him though you were armed only with a sling and some stones from the brook, and your own sublime confidence and courage. Well, old friend, you have need of that same confidence and courage now. And I tell you that Amnon, after this wickedness, is not fit to be King of Israel, for what he did was worse than a crime, it was a blunder, after which no man in Israel can put their trust in him again. You remember how when the black mood came upon Saul, the army trembled and its spirit froze. It will be like that with Amnon. Therefore I urge you to send him into exile, and to name Absalom, whom the army and the young men adore, as your sole heir."

So I was assailed with contradictory advice, and tormented by the stings of reason and sentiment.

Jonadab – who watched over my bedchamber – was now, with Hushai, my chief confidant, and I was grateful to him, since he did not bombard me with advice which I did not wish to hear.

So, since I could not keep words locked up in my heart, I talked with him, though I knew him to be a blabbermouth. And indeed there was some advantage to be had from his loose tongue; it enabled me to disseminate my intentions without proclaiming them openly. "The King," Jonadab would say, "is determined to restore concord in the royal house and the nation. He is fixed in his purpose, he will not alter the succession," and so forth. Meanwhile I trusted to time and patience, old allies.

"Things must be as they may," I said to Jonadab, "which is as the Lord wishes and will provide."

Amnon was for a long time reluctant to be alone with me. He feared my love more than my reproof.

"Guilt and self-loathing are mingled in his soul," Jonadab reported.

Amnon gave himself up to religious exercises and penance. His crime intensified his natural melancholy. He never smiled and, when asked his opinion on any matter, would sigh, lower his eyes, and indicate that he felt that such a man as he, was unworthy of offering a judgement. His humility won him the regard of the priests, and there was a danger in that, for it seemed to me that the house of Israel was divided against itself, the priests favouring Amnon, and the army Absalom. Yet, as long as

Joab was commander-in-chief, under me, the army could not be absolute for my younger son. It irked me to feel that I depended on Joab, but I could not deny that I did.

As time passed, it seemed that my patience was rewarded. Amnon recovered a degree of self-confidence; Absalom behaved to his brother as I would have wished. Though they never met in private, he was polite and respectful to him in council, even ready to defer to him as the heir to the throne.

To me, Absalom was as loving as he had been before Amnon's crime cast a shadow over his spirit. His presence invigorated me and the charm of his manner was a perpetual delight. When therefore he came to me one day and said that he intended to hold a great feast at his new estate of Baal-hazor, at the time of the sheep-shearing, and hoped that I would be one of the company, it cost me much to decline; but I did so because I felt that the presence of the King would impose a certain solemnity on the occasion which would be unwelcome. It is one of the penalties of majesty: on festal occasions people are anxious for the King's departure. So I would not go.

Absalom expressed his disappointment, then said:

"Nevertheless I trust that my brother Amnon will accept my invitation."

"Why should you wish to have him? I know that, although you behave fittingly to him in public, you do not love him."

"No," Absalom said, "I cannot love him. We are made of different matter. And yet he is my father's son, and the heir to the throne. Our estrangement has lasted too long. Moreover, its consequences are dangerous. There are now two parties in the State, or rather two parties among the young men, one favouring me, the other my brother. I do not think this is right; I know it is not what you wish, Father. Therefore I hope Amnon will come as a guest to my house so that I may show all the people that we are at peace together, and that there is no cause for division. So, since Amnon distrusts me, I would be pleased, Father, if you would urge him to come."

I was delighted by the nobility of his sentiments, and agreed to do as he asked. Smiles like a summer morning lit up his face. He swooped towards me, and kissed me on the cheek, then turned and strode, radiant, strong-limbed, and with a grace that cut my heart, away, out of my presence. Oh Absalom, my son, my beloved son, how and where did I fail you?

I was awoken by the cry of women and the running of feet. Pushing my concubine aside, I gathered a robe about me, and left my bedchamber. As I did so, a wild-eyed young man threw himself to the marble floor, and clutched my ankles. He lifted his head and cried:

"Treason and murder! Treason and murder! All the King's sons have been slain and there is not one left alive!"

I do not remember what followed. The ballad-singers have it that I threw myself on the ground and tore my clothes and howled like a dog. I may have done so, but I do not recall it. To hear of such a disaster annihilates memory.

But I remember a moment of terror: why was I still alive myself?

Then I was in my bedchamber. The concubine's eyes were dark, she shook with terror, her mouth opened in a soundless wail. She was naked and trembled to look at me. From the antechamber rose again the wailing of mourning.

I dismissed the girl, and sent to fetch Jonadab. Then I dressed. I remember that. I sat on the end of the bed with a sword held in both hands, point to the ground, and resting between my legs.

I called a woman.

"Is Bathsheba safe? Send to the nursery and see that all is well with Solomon."

At last Jonadab came. He knelt before me and placed his hands on mine gripping the sword-blade.

"It is not as they say," he said. "It is not true that all the King's sons are dead. Only Amnon is dead."

"Absalom?"

"Absalom," he said, "Absalom, my lord king, has revenged himself and his sister Tamar for the wrong she suffered. It was, I fear, long purposed. But only Amnon is dead. He was killed when full of wine, but first Absalom spoke to him."

I thought, even then: how does he know this? He was not there. How does he know?

But I chose not to ask, fearing the answer. If Jonadab was disloyal, where was I to look for loyalty?

"Absalom?" I said.

"Absalom has fled, north, to the land of Geshur, his mother's country."

"Go," I said; but he would not move till he had suffered me to release the sword which I held. When I saw it in his hands, I looked at it with wonder.

So, I lost two sons, and mourned them both, and I turned to the Lord and said:

"And so Uriah the Hittite is revenged. Have mercy on Thy subject, O Lord, and do not visit me with further grief."

25

From Geshur Absalom sent letters justifying his conduct. Time and again he expressed his deep love for me. His words pained me, for I could not read them without seeing his lovely face, hearing his voice, light, caressing and full of the spirit of mockery, and feeling his delightful presence. I longed for him as a lover weeps for his beloved who has gone on a journey and may never return. My heart told me to call out to Absalom and summon him from exile. And yet I did not do so. He was guilty of the sin of Cain, and, even as I read his letters, the pale shade of Amnon's unhappy face seemed to tremble before my gaze. And I prayed to the Lord that He might guide me in the paths of righteousness.

Bathsheba too, I understood, was determined that Absalom should remain in exile.

"The country," she said, "goes quieter without him. I know you love him dearly, David, as of course it is natural that you should, love him all the more, it may be, because he is wild and wayward and, yes, dangerous as an unbroken colt. But when you consider the tranquillity that now prevails in Israel, then I'm sure that you realise that Absalom's absence contributes to that quiet. The truth is, we are all better off without him, and only your love for the boy – your more than reasonable love, your excessive partiality – blinds you to the facts of the matter."

I was powerless against Bathsheba, for she had a capacity to disturb me, and an ability to make my life wretched, that were too strong for me. It is not good for a man to depend on a woman as I did on Bathsheba in those years. She was also increasingly active in the business of government, to Joab's disgust, which did not entirely displease me.

Israel was at peace. Neighbouring kings were happy to pay tribute to my greatness, and the riches they sent me were set aside for my purpose of building a house worthy of the Lord. I recruited and trained architects, stone-carvers, workers in wood and precious stones, so that the work should be done in the most magnificent and seemly manner.

In those years of peace I devoted myself with renewed zeal to poetry and music. I inaugurated a library where collections of verses might be stored, that posterity should wonder at the greatness of the work I had done. I also set Jehoshaphat and Senaiah, scribes, to the work of compiling a history of the Children of Israel, a task never before attempted. I examined the work they had done and had occasion to reprove them for their treatment of Samuel and Saul, and the quarrel that had broken out between them.

"It is natural," I said, "for you as priests to assume that Samuel was in the right, but, though I owe much to him, and though King Saul declared me an enemy of Israel and would have had my life, it was not like that. Saul did his best according to his lights, and Samuel's hatred of Saul had its roots in his jealousy of his achievement, not in any wrongdoing on Saul's part. Believe me, Saul was a great man in Israel and did great things, till his mind became clouded. I pray you, revise these passages, to do justice to both these remarkable men." I am happy to believe that posterity will say I advised wisely.

And all the time I pined for Absalom, and my pleasure in my work was dimmed and tarnished by his absence.

In compensation I spent much time with my next son Adonijah, the son of Haggith, a girl of gentle beauty who had died giving birth to him. Adonijah had much of Absalom's grace and charm, though old women said he resembled me in my own youth. It seemed to me that if Absalom had, to my deepest regret, excluded himself from the succession by his own act, Adonijah must be trained in his place. (But I said nothing of this intention to Bathsheba.) There was another reason for cultivating the boy: Jonadab had reported that Achitophel was doing likewise. Adonijah was given to impulsive, even rash speech – he once in my presence remarked that Solomon was a beastly little two-faced piece of ordure – but he made me laugh and feel younger. Also, and perhaps more to the point, he showed an aptitude for military things which won even Joab's admiration.

Yet I did not name him my successor, because I still hoped for Absalom's return, and because I did not feel strong enough to endure the chilling fury with which I knew that Bathsheba would greet such news.

Moreover, Bathsheba could still delight me more than any other woman when she chose to, and I was tied to her by the twisted ropes of pity, love, lust, and guilt.

One day, a woman craved audience of me. She was dressed in mourning, and threw herself on the ground before me.

"I'm a poor woman," she wailed, "a poor widow woman, and I had two sons, fine boys both of them. But though I loved them both, they did not love each other, and they quarrelled, and the younger killed the elder, and then, fearing for his life, ran away, even while I wept in mourning for his brother. And now the rest of my family, and my husband's family, and the family of my dead son's wife, are urging me to beg the King to seek out my younger son and have him killed as the murderer of his brother. O lord king, my son confesses his guilt, and I confess it to the King, but if he is slain, I shall have no son. His brother is dead and cannot be restored to life, and I am made miserable by the thought that I shall lose my other son and so leave no memory of my husband or myself on the face of the earth. Therefore I beg the King to step in and save my son's life, and restore him to me."

I do not pretend that I have given all her words, or her exact words, for she was voluble, and somewhat confused in her grief and agitation; but the sense of the matter was clear. I felt the love she had for her son, and I promised her I would do as she asked and cast my protection over the boy.

Then she threw back her veil and said,

"O lord king, I have deceived you, for I have no sons, but you have, and the dearest of them languishes in exile, and his life is endangered by his enemies, just like the son in my story. And hearing that, you have judged well and wisely: can you do less than that in the case of your own beloved son, Absalom?"

Then I said: "Do I see Joab's hand in this comedy you have played to me?"

For I knew Joab was jealous of Bathsheba's influence, and I suspected that he believed it would be to his advantage if Absalom was recalled. Yet, because the woman had revealed my own heart to me, I was not angry with Joab. Instead I sent for him, and, letting him know that I had penetrated his device, smiled, and told him to fetch Absalom from exile.

"The Lord knoweth my iniquities" – I have sung that song often. "The Lord seeth my secret heart . . ." And so on. It is true, I believe it. But it is one thing to walk naked before the Lord; another to strip oneself in the sight of men. And yet, if in these last days I am to tell the whole truth about myself, that is what I must now do. I must uncover my shame.

(O Abishag, come naked as the dawn, and kiss my withered lips, revive me with your soft mouth and cunning hands, that, in this extremity, I may think – no, feel – myself a man again!)

Almost all men would rather confess to wrongdoing than to weakness, and in this respect at least, I am no different from the common run. There may be a grandeur in wrongdoing; it is at least an act, an expression of the will, and often, the will to power, that food which restores vitality, and quickens the appetite it feeds on. But weakness is an abnegation of the will; weakness is always to be despised. And that is what I must confess to.

Bathsheba came to me and her smile seemed painted on her lips and cold as the desert night.

"And so," she said, "Absalom is to return. Your beloved son the murderer is to be received with joy – and I was not even consulted. Is he to be free to murder Solomon now or perhaps Adonijah – "

"Bathsheba," I said, "please."

But she continued in this vein, tearing at me like one of those little dogs that farmers keep to kill rats.

"I thought you loved me," she cried. "You have often boasted of your love for me. And now I see what it is worth – mere words."

In other moods (as she would have me believe): "To do this without consulting me, that is what hurts," she wailed.

Then again: "Everyone at court knows that I have opposed Absalom's return. When I have been asked, I have not hesitated to give my opinion. And now you will shame me before all the people, and make a mock of me."

Or: "Do you believe that Absalom loves you? How could he do so when he slew Amnon your firstborn son? Was that the way in which a boy shows his love for his father?"

When I put my hand to her face, and touched her lips as I used to do, or laid it on her breasts, she turned away and denied herself to me.

"No," she cried, "you have won me by soft words and loving ways before, and now I know it was all a cheat. Was it for this that I turned from my rightful husband, Uriah, and invited censure for love of you, and gravely offended my grandfather Achitophel, that you should now reward me by shaming me . . .

"David," she said in tears, "David" – she spoke in a soft lingering moan, "David, if you love me, you would not treat me in this way. Well, I have been a fool. I prized your love, it was the sunshine in the summer of my life, and now I see it was but a means of winning me, of proving your power, of rendering me subject to your monstrous will. For your sake, I suffered the scorn of women, I allowed myself to be branded whore, and I endured that because I believed you loved me."

I thought: I sinned for your sake. I murdered Uriah for your sake. I made myself outcast from the love of the Almighty for your sake. And now . . .

But I could not speak these words. She was too strong for me. I had stood against Goliath, I had stood against Saul, I had trampled the hosts of the Philistines under my feet, but when Bathsheba turned her face to the wall, and denied me, my will became as water.

"Very well," I said. "I shall not rescind my decision that Absalom shall return. It is too late for that, and would arouse discontent. But he shall not see my face. He shall be excluded from the palace and confined to his own house in the suburbs of the city. Will that satisfy you?"

Then she hung on my lips, and gave herself to me with sweet words; and I knew delight again, but even at the height of my passion despised myself because I had allowed my wife to govern me.

26

For two years I kept my vow. Absalom addressed protests and pleas to me, but I had given my word to Bathsheba and was not inclined to break it. Yet all the time I was wretched. My pleasures seemed to me stale and profitless. I was loth to leave my bed in the morning and eager to seek it at night, though for the first time since I was a boy I mostly occupied it without any companion.

When I looked at Bathsheba I often caught an expression in her eye, which seemed to measure me, as if she was judging how long I would last, and how soon the crown might pass to Solomon. Once, not long before, I would have been distressed to see how much deeper was her love for her son than for me. Now it was a matter of indifference.

To my surprise Achitophel concurred in the decision I had reached – that Absalom be kept from me.

"You know," he said, "that I have an affection for the lad. Who can fail to respond to his charm? Yet, David, I am an old man who has served Israel all his life, and I believe you have found something of merit in my counsel. And I am sorry to have to say that for all his qualities Absalom is too rash, too impetuous, to be king. You would do better to settle the succession on Solomon."

Nevertheless, Hushai reported that Achitophel cultivated Absalom's society, and that of the young men who congregated about him.

"The old fox has some game in play," he said.

I thought: I care nothing for any of it.

One winter night when there was no moon, and the wind from the mountains rattled the rooftops of Jerusalem, I found myself black as the starless sky. I drank wine, joylessly, and envied Joab who sought refuge from care and disappointment in intoxication. I thought: I have served the Lord all my life, I have done great things for Israel, and now my grey hairs are descending in misery to the grave. The days of darkness have come upon me, and all my mighty deeds are vanity.

"My God, my God," I cried, "why hast Thou forsaken me? O, my God, I cry in the daytime, but Thou hearest not, and in the night season, I am not silent."

Then I thought: Absalom and the young men may mock me, because I am governed by a woman.

So I sent for Jonadab, and when he came, I gave him wine to drink, and asked him what men now said of me.

He gazed at the ground and would not answer.

"Tell me," I said, "do you know the house where Absalom is to be found, and could you guide me to it secretly?"

So I put on a cloak, and covered my face with its folds, and Jonadab led me out into the city. We kept to the narrow streets like thieves, and dogs barked at us. We passed taverns from which came sounds of revelry, in which I heard no merriment. Yet as we continued, I felt my black mood lift from me. It was as if I had shaken myself free from the bonds of kingship, and my youth was renewed.

"If any greet us," I whispered to my companion, "remember that I am not the King, but a traveller from a distant land."

And indeed I felt like such a traveller, and this exhilarated me.

We were challenged at the gate to Absalom's house. I held back, while Jonadab negotiated our entry. For a moment I hesitated. I had no wish to break in on a company of my son's friends.

"I must see the young man alone," I whispered.

So I was left in an antechamber while Jonadab went in search of Absalom. I waited like a poor client, and found myself as fearful as such a client must often feel, for I did not know how Absalom would receive the news of my presence.

Then the curtain was swept aside, and he was with me. His face was flushed. He fell on his knees before me, and grasped mine. I raised him up and kissed him, and held him in my arms, and for a long time we did not speak, but I knew peace.

We talked the night away. Much that we said was insignificant. Much has slipped my failing memory. Things were said, I am sure, which are better forgotten. Then he assured me of his deep love for me, and of his lack of resentment. I begged his forgiveness, he mine.

He said: "I have been so tempted to despair. I thought you had abandoned me. I thought you had cast me into utter darkness."

"My dear," I said, "I have been dwelling in the valley of despair myself. But despair is forbidden us. Despair is a sin against a loving God."

"I have seen little sign of the love of God," he said; and it seemed to me that in those words he accused me with an unquenchable bitterness.

Then he said, "There is one . . . thing . . . I must show you."

I followed him through long and winding passages. Our way was lit only by the lamp that he carried, and then we descended a flight of stairs into the cold depths of his house. He took a key from his belt and unlocked a metal-studded door. We passed through it and into a long dank corridor. For a moment I was afraid, suspecting that Absalom – even my son – intended me harm. The place was so like a prison.

Sensing my hesitation, he took me by the arm, but said nothing.

We passed through another door, this one unlocked, and came into a little room, lit only by a single oil-lamp. An old crone sat, sewing, on a three-legged stool, by an iron-barred gate which gave on to an inner room. She looked up, and her jowls shook when she recognised me. Absalom laid his hand on her wrist.

"I have brought my father to see my sister. How is she today?"

"She was restive, sir, in the way she is which you know well, moaning and crying out for the first part of the night, and would have torn at her face had I not bound her hands. But now she sleeps, not soundly, because her sleep, as you know, sir, is ever unquiet, but such sleep as she is granted, she has enjoyed."

I peered through the iron grille. A shape lay on a pallet

bed, but I could not discern whether it was man, woman, or even beast.

"Tamar . . ." I said. "But you sent word from Geshur that she was dead."

"It would be better if she were," he said. "She would have it that way herself. She has many times attempted her life, and I have prevented her. Perhaps I have been wrong, but then I have never despaired of her recovery. Tamar, my darling," he called her in the most gentle of voices.

He called again, and a third time. Then the girl rose from the bed, and moved towards us, with a strange gliding motion, as if she had been a spirit, and not flesh. She was dressed only in a soiled and ragged tunic or shift, of saffron yellow in that shadowy light. Her face was scarred, as if with old knife-strokes, and streaked with dirty tears. Her eyes were wild, and yet distant, but the long hair was combed. Her mouth hung open and, when she saw Absalom, she babbled, strange sounds that I could not interpret, the language of a beast rather than a woman.

She seized Absalom's hands through the bars of the gate, and pressed her lips against them.

I could not speak, but turned away in misery.

"You see, Father," Absalom said, when we had departed from that scene of horror, and made our dolorous way back to the chamber where he had first received me, "you see, Father, she wears the semblance of a monster. She has to be confined, for her own sake."

"It would have been better if she had died."

"That is so," he said. "She has moments of lucidity, and these are the worst times, for then she remembers what she was, and knows what she is now."

"She did not know me," I said.

"She knows only me, and Anna, the old woman who cares for her."

I thought: what sin has brought this on me?

"Absalom," I said, "I have wronged you. I have been weak, and have listened to those who do not love you, and have been persuaded by Bathsheba to do you wrong. The Lord has revealed to me the evil that I have done, and I am truly sorry and filled with penitence."

So we embraced and, accompanied by Jonadab prattling his joy at the way things had turned out, I returned in the grey-pink light of dawn to the palace.

In the morning I announced that Absalom had restored himself to my favour, and should now take his rightful place in the government of Israel.

A leader can have no equals, no friends, and must give his confidence to no one, nor allow intrusions into the intimacies of his existence. I saw that I had erred by permitting Bathsheba too much influence over me, and therefore determined henceforth to keep her at a distance. Privately, I told Jonadab to convey to her my wish that she should be denied access to me.

Absalom's return restored to my rule a popularity that it had been in danger of losing. Jonadab now felt bold enough to let me know how deeply Bathsheba had been resented by my councillors and how unpopular she had become with the people. Public opinion is of course a harlot, easily swayed and without principle; nevertheless the wise leader wishes to cultivate and direct it. I now learned from Hushai's agents how deep disaffection had run. They told me of conspiracies hatched among the northern tribes, and I acted quickly to suppress them and to punish the guilty.

Absalom was eager that I should name him my heir. All my loving instincts urged me to gratify him by such an announcement; and yet I held back from doing so. To appease him, I told him that I wished to protect him against the jealousy which such an announcement would breed, and that I did not wish to make him in particular the object of Bathsheba's hatred.

"Bathsheba is determined," I said, "that Solomon will succeed me as king . . . let her dream her dreams, we shall all be quieter as a result. Solomon is only a studious youth with no experience of war. I do not think that when I die you will have any difficulty with him. Meanwhile, my dear son, let me enjoy peace in my old age. I still love Bathsheba, though for your sake I have ordered her to be kept from me for the time being. You will know how to deal with Solomon when the time comes."

The truth was more complicated. I was conscious that with the advance of years went a decline of bodily and mental vigour, and I feared that to name a successor might make some think that it was time for me to be supplanted. I had no doubts as to Absalom's love and loyalty, but I could not feel so certain about some of those around him. So I preferred to keep this nomination in reserve, so that there should be two rival parties in the State, each uncertain of the other, and each still looking to me for security.

But to appease Absalom, and to demonstrate the trust I put in him, I made him governor over Judah, my home country where loyalty to me was, as I thought – O too trustfully – absolute.

And when he was gone to take up residence at Hebron, with many expressions of love and gratitude, I was confident that I had acted wisely.

Meanwhile I had had Tamar brought to the palace, and lodged there as befitted a king's daughter. Alas, she went into a decline, and shortly after Absalom departed for Hebron, refused to eat, and died. It was pitiful to see.

Her funeral was celebrated with the utmost magnificence, with a display of popular grief.

Bathsheba continued to address me letters of reproach; berating me for my cruelty and, as she thought, dishonesty. I replied that she had tried to turn me against my beloved son Absalom, that she had tempted me to an act of great wickedness, and that if she continued to plague me in this manner, I would have her charged with witchcraft. Then I ordered that she and Solomon should remove themselves from Jerusalem, and take up residence in Shiloh, for I was wearied of them.

And so I prepared myself a comfortable old age, in which the cares of government would rest lightly on my shoulders, and I would cultivate the arts, and prepare my soul to meet my Maker.

27

I am sure Absalom loved me. Yet, when he was not with me, he listened to the words of my enemies. Some of them were men who owed much to me, as indeed all Israel did. The chief among them was Achitophel, and his motives still puzzle me. We had worked together, and I had always paid him honour. I admired his subtle intelligence, and had given him high office. But something in him rebelled against my greatness. The canker of resentment ate at his soul. Accustomed all his life to thinking himself more intelligent than all others, and in the habit likewise of dwelling on his intelligence to compensate for his complete lack of military prowess, he had long affected to despise soldiers, even while in reality envying them. Joab and he had been at perpetual enmity, which did not displease me; but Achitophel was comfortable in that enmity, for he never doubted his superiority to Joab. This was foolish of him, for in certain respects Joab was his master; but I have often observed that the very clever are also inclined to foolishness. Only clever men for instance deny God, though stupid ones may forget him.

Achitophel felt himself diminished by me.

Bathsheba had also suggested that though he was her grand-father, his reason for opposing our marriage was not only, as I supposed, because he had not himself suggested it, or formed the scheme; and not because he felt any affection for Uriah, though he was the Hittite's patron; but, vilely, because he nursed an incestuous passion for her.

"He dare not confess it," she said, "but I have seen his eyes devour me. They have stripped the gown from my body, and feasted themselves on my nakedness."

Yet, though I knew Achitophel's sentiments, I was not anxious when word was brought me that he was constant in attendance on Absalom. I trusted in my son's love, and I knew that he could learn much from one as experienced in statecraft as Achitophel. Even when Joab approached me and said that in his view treachery was being plotted, I was not alarmed. Joab, I thought, was jealous.

Looking back, it seems to me as if black velvet covered my eyes, so intense was the darkness in which I moved. In which, indeed, I chose to move.

There are moments even when I wonder if I did not will what happened.

On a brisk morning in early summer I was bathing when Jonadab burst into my chamber, and cried:

"The trumpets have sounded over all Israel, and Absalom has been proclaimed king in Hebron."

It was as if the light of the Almighty had been extinguished.

Jonadab, seeming to fear that my silence indicated that I had not understood, said again;

"Absalom has been proclaimed king in Hebron, and all Judah is in revolt."

"But Judah is mine," I said.

"Judah is Absalom's – all the young men's hearts are with him."

I made no reply, but called my slaves to dress me. While they did so, and scented my beard, all of which was done with the slow formality of court, I tried to gather my thoughts.

First: this was the end; the Lord had forsaken me.

Then: Achitophel was behind this; he was acting in Absalom's name.

I said to Jonadab: "Send to Absalom, and ask him on what terms he will accept my submission. Will he spare my life?"

Jonadab did not move. His body seemed to stiffen. It was as if he said, "I did not hear your words, O King."

I thought: how pleased Bathsheba will be.

I said: "What forces are left to us?"

"That's better," Jonadab said. "I don't know. I'll find out."

"It doesn't matter. We are finished. I'm finished. The comedy is over."

"My lord king, you don't know what you are saying."

"No, you're right. I don't."

I ordered him to summon a council.

"At least we'll see which of my generals and ministers have not deserted me."

Throughout this memoir I have told nothing but the truth. I wish now I had entrusted it to another, or stopped it earlier, for to confront the truth of that morning is terrible.

All my life danger has stimulated me, and quickened my spirit and my wits. But I was then as one prostrated by a paralysis of the will.

And I knew fear. I asked myself what death Achitophel had planned for me.

I remembered how the Lord had turned against me and my house because I had been guilty of the death of Uriah.

"O Lord," I cried, "do not bring down Thy servant's grey head in sorrow to the grave."

I entered the council chamber leaning on Jonadab's shoulder, and saw fear in every face, save Joab's.

I said: "All my life I have served Israel and the Lord of Hosts, who has deserted me in my old age."

I sank into a chair, and gestured to Joab, inviting him to speak. But I could scarce follow his words. They rolled over me like the wind. I saw only Absalom's face, bright-eyed and loving, and a tremor shook my hand. Others talked, and still I could not bring myself either to listen, or to intervene, or to depart. Arguments clashed like swords over my bowed head, and I smelled fear. Then Joab pounded the table with the flat of his hand.

"Enough," he shouted. "Rebellion must be met with force, immediately, before it spreads. I shall therefore gather my guard, and march south against Hebron. I have no doubt that we shall collect more troops and reinforcements on the march, and scatter the rebels and leave their bodies as food for the fowls of the air, the birds of death."

I lifted my head.

"No," I said.

"No," I said again. "We shall run away. We shall abandon Jerusalem."

"David," Joab said, and I heard exasperation in his voice, "you know the strength of the city's defences. I shall leave a sufficient garrison, and if my attack is checked then I shall fall back on the city, which can withstand a longer siege than I guess the rebels will be capable of maintaining."

"No," I said, again, but this time with decision, for Joab's words had had at least this result: they had recalled me to myself.

"Jerusalem is a trap," I said. "Joab, you remember Keilah, and how Saul was delighted when he believed we would defend ourselves there."

It was as if the clouds had dissolved to reveal the hard clear shape of mountains. I could not trust that Joab would defeat Absalom's forces if he marched against them – and if he failed, we were destroyed. I could not trust the loyalty of the populace of Jerusalem, or rely on their willingness to endure the hardships of a siege. I feared that the rebellion would spread to the northern tribes, among whom were many who had accepted my reign only on sufferance. It seemed to me therefore that I must stiffen their loyalty, and there was no surer way of doing that than by coming among them with my army.

And so I said, "We shall run away and leave Jerusalem to Absalom," though I knew my motives would be misunderstood, and that many would think me the victim of fear; and in truth the fear was there, alert and disquieting.

I sent a message to Bathsheba in Shiloh, urging her to collect troops and hold them at my disposal.

I said: "You were wiser than I, in your judgement."

They were bitter words to write, but necessary.

I gave orders to Joab to make ready to march out of the city to the north.

Then I dismissed the council, only requiring Hushai to remain with me.

"I have a difficult and dangerous task for you, my friend."

"I am yours to command."

"I want you," I said, "to remain in the city. When the young man enters it, you will go to him and honour him as king. You will promise to serve him as faithfully as you have served me, and then you will use your wisdom to confound the counsels of Achitophel. In this way, I shall have a friend among the enemy, and we shall devise a means by which you can inform me of what is intended."

I knew that this was a heavy weight to place upon Hushai, for I feared, as he must himself have feared, that Achitophel would suspect his protestations, and persuade Absalom that Hushai was a spy. Yet, he consented without hesitation. It was one of the noblest tributes ever paid to me.

We arranged that he should find a way to communicate with me through Zadok and Abiathar, the High Priests whom I also commanded to remain in the city.

"The Ark of the Covenant of the Lord," I told them, "must remain in Jerusalem, which is the city I have dedicated to the Lord."

I had two reasons for this decision. In the first place, I had no desire that we should be burdened by the need to protect the Ark; second, I knew that my order that it should remain in Jerusalem would impress waverers with my certainty that I should return.

Yet, as our little cavalcade trooped out of the city as the shades of evening fell, and news came to us that Absalom's advance guard was but three miles from the southern gates, my heart was heavy, and my thoughts bitter. I was again all but overcome by lassitude, and the temptation to turn back and submit to Absalom, requesting only that he spare the lives of my friends and permit me to retire to a holy place, and live my last days in the service of the Lord, was powerful. "I have had enough of blood" – the refrain sang in my ears. I turned back, and saw the sun lie red on the city's western wall, and I gazed to the north and saw the immensity of an uncertain future stretch before me across the sands of time; and I all but wept at the pity of it.

It was only the thought of Achitophel's triumph, and the image of his face gloating over my humiliation, that prevented me from throwing up the game.

But that Absalom could have surrendered his judgement and his love to Achitophel's soft words of sedition cut me to the heart. Truly, I thought, the old man's words were softer than oil, and yet were they also an unsheathed sword.

We advanced beyond the Mount of Olives as the night closed upon us. But I would not suffer our little force to rest there, though my own limbs were weary, and the turmoil of the day had rendered me feeble almost to the point of tears. Instead, I commanded Joab, who sat rock-like and grim on his horse, to press on, though I myself was now so weak that I required a litter.

Towards first light we descended to Bahurim, by a path which leads to a ford across the Jordan. Then a cry came from the rocks, and looking up I saw a figure there, an old man whom I recognised as Shimei, an enemy of mine and a cousin of Saul.

He cried out to me,

"And is this you, David, the enemy of my house, in cowardly flight from your own son? Run, run, you man of blood and son of Belial, for I see that your unworthy son of an unworthy father is the agent of the Lord, who this day has repaid you for shedding the blood of the house of Saul. The Lord has delivered the kingdom into the hand of your son, your most beloved son, Absalom. You are caught in your own wickedness, drowned in the blood which you have shed."

Then he cackled, most horribly, like the madman that he was.

Abishai riding beside me turned to me with a face as grim as on that night when he had accompanied me to Saul's tent and urged me to slay the King.

"Why should this dog curse the King, and why will the King tolerate it? Let me go, I beg you, up that rock and take his head from his shoulders, that all Israel may learn that no man may insult the King with impunity."

I was tempted to consent, for the hatred which Shimei directed at me aroused in me a strong desire to see him dead. But we were now in the land of Benjamin. Shimei, mad as he might be, vile as he certainly was, was also of the tribe of Benjamin, of the family of Saul, and had a wide connection. To kill him would be a pleasure, and might impress some with my determination. But it might rouse others against me, who would say that David goes about the land slaying all like a mad wolf; it is time to put a stop to him.

So I said instead to Abishai: "Let him be. The man is mad. So he curses me. His curses are light and easy to bear in a day when my own son has risen against me and seeks to destroy me and kill me. Let him be, and let him curse, for nothing he says can wound me more than I have been wounded already."

And so we rode on, pursued by his curses, and came to the bank of the Jordan. I drank some wine, as Joab marshalled our men to cross. The word came that Bathsheba was approaching with a small force, and I looked towards the north from which she was coming; but in my mind's eye I saw only Absalom in his beauty, and I struggled to understand how he had allowed himself to be turned against his loving father.

28

Absalom was received in Jerusalem with all the enthusiasm of which a fickle and ungrateful populace was capable. This news I had from Hushai, by way of two young men, Jonathan and Ahimaaz, the sons of the priests Zadok and Abiathar.

As soon as he had acknowledged the welcome, Absalom summoned one of the concubines I had left in the palace, and took possession of her, by Achitophel's advice, in sight of the people, as proof that he was king in my place.

"Moreover," Hushai suggested, "Achitophel believes that such a public insult to you will prove unpardonable, and so make it impossible for Absalom to turn his hand from the rebellion which, I must assure you, is entirely the work of his evil counsellor."

How little Achitophel understood the depths of a father's love for an errant son!

Then there was a debate on the course of action to be pursued. According to Hushai, Achitophel was clear in his advice. The King had withdrawn from the city, he said, but he had not surrendered the throne to Absalom. The King was an old fox, cunning in warfare. By leaving Jerusalem, he had surprised them, and Absalom must not suppose that his father's nerve had failed. No, it was part of a plan. David had retired merely to mobilise his forces and recruit new ones, and to strengthen his army. He must not be given time to do so. Otherwise Absalom and his followers might find themselves compelled to give battle at a time of David's choosing and at a place of defence selected by him. "No man," Achitophel said, "has ever had a better eye for country than David or greater skill in defensive warfare. And he still has Joab with him, the most experienced man of war that Israel has ever known, and the finest trainer of an army." Therefore Achitopel urged that they waste no time, but set out in pursuit with all the forces they could muster, and so crush our little band while we were still disheartened and unprepared.

Hushai immediately realised that Achitophel's advice was good, and that if it was followed, we would be destroyed. (He was wise in that judgement.) Yet Absalom, to his joy and relief, hesitated, he could not say why. (I like to think that, though Absalom had been brought to this point by the evil and dishonest wiles of Achitophel, he was still restrained by his love for me, and could not bring himself to embark on a course of action which would destroy me utterly. Perhaps, too, he still hoped that I would submit. At any rate, he could not bring himself to look reality, with its stark imperatives, in the face.)

Hushai, seeing Absalom's hesitation, cleared his throat, and asked modestly (by his account) whether he might give his opinion.

"Much as I respect Achitophel, and have always been accustomed to defer to his judgement," he said, "this time I dissent. His advice is not good for he has permitted his very natural wish to bring things to a successful conclusion to dictate his thought."

Consider, Hushai went on when he was certain he had the attention of the company, the facts of the case. (I could imagine Achitophel frown with irritation as he heard Hushai pronounce this mild but specious sentence.) David and Joab were the two greatest captains of the age. The force with them might be small, but it was composed of veterans who had shared so many triumphs, and who would now die to the last man rather than submit to defeat. "Battle," Hushai said, "is terrible and its outcome never certain." He advised instead consolidation of their position.

This report brought a bitter smile to my lips. "Consolidation" is a word that ever attracts the timid, and comforts their apprehension.

Instead of risking all on one uncertain encounter, Hushai

suggested, Absalom should instead muster his support from the northern tribes, so that the fugitive King would recognise the hopelessness of his position, and his army would lose heart.

Achitophel protested, but the opinion of the council was in Hushai's favour, and Absalom accepted the decision of the majority.

I like to think that he was pleased to do so, for I cannot believe that he really wished to engage me in battle.

When this news was brought to us, Joab slapped the flat of his broadsword, and cried out that the Lord was still with us.

"Great is His name," he shouted, "for He has made our enemy mad."

And so we crossed Jordan unopposed and established ourselves in the Forest of Ephraim.

I myself then withdrew sick at heart into the town of Mahanaim, whence I sent messages to all the chief men in Israel, even to those who had acknowledged Absalom as king, recalling them to their duty and obedience. I hoped that I might be able to induce a sufficient number of them to desert Absalom, so that he himself would recognise the folly of his rebellion, and surrender himself to me. Then I sent a message to Hushai, by a secret route, instructing him to sow this seed in my son's heart. But, alas, he found he could not do so without putting himself at risk; and this is the sole reproach I have to levy at Hushai concerning his conduct in this terrible time.

I was grieved to learn also that my nephew Amasa had deserted me to join his cousin Absalom, and was still more perturbed to hear that he had been made commander of the rebel army. Amasa was a young man whom I myself had schooled in the art of war, and I feared he might prove a good pupil.

Meanwhile Joab devoted himself to training our army for the forest warfare with which in general Israelites are unfamiliar. For I had determined that we should stand our ground in Ephraim, and invite the enemy to come upon us.

As for myself, I felt too wretched to take an active part in the preparations. Though I knew how action is a remedy for a heart that is sore and a spirit that is bowed, yet I was afflicted with a strange lassitude, which made me lie long in bed after the sun had risen, and impaired my ability to concentrate.

I thought, many times: this is a war which I should be content to lose.

Often I considered abandoning the struggle, and surrendering to Absalom. I said to myself: he is your beloved son, the heir to the throne, the adored of Israel. Why not yield to him and pass the evening of your days in idle peace?

I said to myself: it is the will of the Lord. One generation passes away, and another generation treads behind it, but the earth abides for ever. I have done great deeds, and I sought wisdom, and it is as the crackling of thorns under a pot: all is vanity and vexation of spirit.

Bathsheba sent Solomon, her son, to me, and it seemed as if his eye measured me for my grave-cloth.

"Well," I said to him, "and will you go to the army?"

"No, Father," he said, "you have soldiers to do your fighting. You understand, Father, that my brother Absalom must die?"

"What do you say?"

"I say what every wise man knows. I say what every true friend of ours believes."

"These are your mother's words," I said, and dismissed him.

And when he was gone I cried out to the Lord as my rock and my salvation.

"Pull me out of the net that my enemies have laid privily for me," I prayed; but I could not determine who were my enemies.

At night, under the stars, I looked from the rooftops towards Jerusalem, where the young man Absalom lodged – thinking what thoughts?

And I would not have Bathsheba by me, but took instead a concubine, the daughter of a tavern-keeper in the town, and lay with her, to silence thought. But when she slept, thoughts returned; and as I sank insensibly into the brief snatches of sleep which were granted me, it was Absalom's face I saw, Absalom's eyes that were fixed on me with a look in which I read judgement, condemnation and pity; and then I woke again, weeping.

* * *

The day came when a message was sent by Hushai to say that Absalom and Amasa were marshalling their forces, and now purposed to march against us.

"It is no longer possible to restrain him," he said.

"Good," said Joab, "the men are ready for battle."

He outlined his dispositions.

"Yes," I said, "yes, I am sure you have done all, that all is ready."

"David," he said, and continued to expound his plan.

"Yes," I said, "the fruit on that fig-tree there is ripe to be plucked and I am sure you will do so."

"This night, we shall sup in Jerusalem," he said.

"Joab," I said, "you will see to it that the young man Absalom comes to no harm."

It is a strange thing to remain in a city within an hour's march of an army engaged in battle, and to know nothing. I looked towards the forest, and there was silence in the heat of the day. They urged me to eat and drink, but I waved them away, and kept my gaze fixed on the forest, in the distant dark. The shadow of the city walls crept before me as the sun sank, and no news came. I felt behind me, within the city, the trembling of fear. For a long time no one approached me, and no one spoke.

Then a cry was raised from the gate, and someone came to me and said that a figure could be seen coming towards us.

"One man? One man alone? Then it is a messenger, not a fugitive from the battle."

A little later, they came again and said a second figure had been sighted, at a distance from the other.

"If he is alone also, then he too is a messenger, and the victory is ours."

I heard a murmuring of relief rise from the crowded streets as the word ran round that the King had spoken, and all was well. Then cheering broke out, and my name was praised most loudly by those who had been held from rebellion only by the fear occasioned by my presence and that of my army. They would have hanged me from the town gate and given my flesh to be food for the fowls of the air, if a cloud of dust had disclosed our soldiers in flight.

So, knowing that my men had won a battle which I would as soon have lost – if defeat could have assured me rest – I withdrew into the house I had taken as my abode, and commanded that the messenger should be brought to me there.

I said to myself: no victory can expel from my mind the memory of my flight from Jerusalem, and what I learned then of the hatred with which men regard me. And I thought: shall I not expunge that hatred with the blood shed in sweet revenge? But another voice sounded in my weary mind: "Vengeance is mine, saith the Lord."

When the messenger approached I recognised him as Ahimaaz, the son of Abiathar the priest, who had served as Hushai's courier from Jerusalem. He fell to the ground before me, his comely face streaming with sweat, and cried out:

"Blessed be the Lord God of Israel who has delivered the King's enemies into His hand, and brought Israel out of darkness."

I thanked him, fittingly, and sent one to convey the news to the city.

"Is all well with the young man Absalom?" I said.

Ahimaaz lowered his head, and spoke in a low voice.

"My lord king, when Joab despatched the King's servant to bear word of the King's victory, there was a great tumult around him, but I know not what it was . . ."

At that moment the second messenger was led into the chamber. I recognised him as an Ethiopian slave belonging to Joab's own household.

"Is all well with the young man Absalom?"

"The enemies of my lord the King, and all that rise up in war against him, be as that young man is."

I withdrew further, into an inner room, and surrendered myself to grief.

Oh Absalom, my son, my son, would God I had died for you, Absalom, my son, my son. From this day there is only darkness, and joy is banished even from the mountain tops.

After a long time I sent for the Ethiopian and commanded that he tell me how Absalom had died.

"Caught in an oak tree and stabbed by Joab."

I gave him gold because he had brought me the bitter news I feared and longed to hear. I might equally have had him lashed, but there was more scorn in a gift of gold. Then I commanded that there be no joy in the city, but respect for the King's grief.

The night fell, and sleep was denied me. I dismissed my concubine who had thought to comfort me, and sat in the cold dark, and called on the Lord to show me the sin for which He had inflicted this punishment upon me.

I thought: no man has won more glory in Israel than I; no man has performed greater deeds; I have made a nation before the Lord from quarrelling tribes; and now in old age I taste the fruit of bitterness.

And I thought also of Saul, and of how the Lord had deserted him likewise, and driven him to the extremity of reason, even beyond it, to consorting with those who practised witchcraft, as he sought comfort in his utter despair.

Then the curtain behind which I concealed myself from the eyes of men was torn aside, and Joab stood before me, stained with the dirt of battle, and in his right hand the drawn sword with which he had killed my son.

"Are you mourning for the brave men who died for you today, David? We have won a mighty victory over your enemies, and I have come in triumph expecting to see you rejoicing and to receive your thanks. And what do I find? The King weeping like a woman, and all the city tell me it is on account of your son, the traitor who rose against you and would have taken your life and throne, had not I, Joab, prevented him. Would the King, unworthy in his womanly weeping of that name, have rather that his brave and loyal army be destroyed so that his unworthy son should live? If so, David, why, I should not have risked my life on your behalf, and nor should the brave men who fought for you. We should all have stayed in bed, and let the King be taken, an object of contempt and mockery. Would you rather that had happened? There are women in this city this night who have cause to weep. They are the mothers, wives, and sweethearts of brave men who died that you might still be king. Does the King comfort them? No, he weeps for the wretch who was the cause of their deaths.

"David, all your life, you have tried my patience hard; yet no man has stood more loyally by you. But there is a limit to all loyalty, even mine. What will your brave soldiers say when they learn that you would rather they had died, to preserve the life of Absalom? Will they not cry out, 'David has rejected us who fought on his behalf. Therefore why should we not reject David as king?' Well, it is not too late to prevent this. They will understand that you mourn the death of your son, even if there is not a man in the army that does not welcome it, not one who is not filled with gratitude that the Lord fought on our side today and that Absalom will no longer disturb the peace of Israel. But they will only do so if you appear before them tomorrow, and express your gratitude to the army, and proclaim a festival of thanksgiving for our deliverance from rebellion and civil war."

I submitted to his brutal reason, though his presence afflicted me with bitterness.

Joab however was premature in supposing the rebellion to be at an end. Amasa, showing that precocious military skill which had caused me to mark him out as a future general of Israel, even when he first served me as an aide-de-camp, contrived to regroup and rally the defeated army, so that it was enabled to withdraw in good order into Jerusalem.

Joab was all for marching immediately on the city, and storming its walls. But I said, "There has been enough blood shed, and besides, the fortifications of Jerusalem which I built are strong, and the army within will be desperate and will not readily submit." So I forbade him, and took pleasure in doing so.

Instead, I sent a message by Ahimaaz to his father Abiathar, and Zadok, the High Priests, who were still within Jerusalem guarding the Ark of the Covenant as I had commanded them, and instructed them to talk with Amasa, and offer a pardon to all engaged in the rebellion, if they would lay down their arms and surrender to me. And I added:

"You will tell the young man that I shall have a special care for him as the friend of his cousin, my son Absalom, whose death has distressed me and whom I mourn every hour of every day."

Amasa understood the wisdom of what I offered, and came himself to me to offer his sword and beg my forgiveness. When I had received him publicly, I said I wished to speak to him in private.

At first we spoke of Absalom, whom we had both loved, and we wept and embraced and comforted each other in our grief.

Then I said: "There is only one other condition, my dear. You must surrender Achitophel to me, that I may punish him for the evil he has done by seducing my son and leading him to disaster."

Amasa pushed back his lustrous curls, and shook his head slowly.

"Achitophel has escaped you. When word came of our defeat, he rode south from Jerusalem to his own estates, and his own house, and there, having put his affairs in order, he threw a rope over a beam, and made a noose, and hanged himself."

I said: "I would that he had not escaped me. A wicked man in the end. His words were softer than fine oil, and yet they drew swords from their scabbards.

"Now," I continued, "I wish, dear boy, to restore peace in Israel. You still command the men of Judah, and after the account you have given of the retreat from Ephraim and your skill in war, I have decided that the best means of effecting the necessary reconciliation will be to place you in command of the army of all Israel. What do you say?"

He was overwhelmed. Despite the assurances Abiathar and Zadok had given him, he had come to meet me in fear and trepidation, for he could not believe that my magnanimity could extend to sparing the life of one who had taken so prominent a part in the rebellion. I had sensed his apprehension, even while I held him in my arms as we lamented Absalom; and for this reason was the more drawn to him, admiring the courage with which he had striven to conceal his fear.

But now he raised the objection which was natural. What of Joab, he asked.

I said: "Joab will as ever submit to my will."

To convince him, I said: "Joab knows that I have never forgotten his murder of Abner, and he knows that I have it in my power to bring him to trial and have him put to death for that crime. And he knows also now that nothing remains to deter me from doing so, since he slew Absalom against my expressed command."

I did not know as I spoke what I have subsequently, and bitterly, learned: that authority deserts a dying king. At the first opportunity, Joab, acting with the same ruthlessness which he had ever shown, murdered Amasa, stabbing him, as he had stabbed Abner and Absalom, with his own sword.

29

When they brought me word that Amasa had been killed, I felt nothing, I could not weep.

I thought: I have served the Lord all my days, and in my last, when I am weak, He visits me with affliction.

A voice sounded in my ear: "Curse God and die."

And I wondered why I should not do so, since all conspired to deceive me and bring me pain: Absalom, whom I loved better than glory, had sought to kill me; Amasa, whom I had chosen to be my stay in my last days, had been brutally snatched from me, by Joab, whom I had long hated, and who – I now saw – returned that hatred with an added measure.

I thought of the hours of love-making with Bathsheba, and now my flesh stank.

I remembered the words of Shimei as I fled before Absalom: "You are caught in your own wickedness and drowning in the blood which you have shed."

And yet I have done nothing but what I had to.

Jonadab came to me, wriggling his backside, squirming with delight as the bearer of ill news. He spoke to me of betrayal, of how he had surprised Abishag with my son Adonijah.

I said: "They are young, and I am old. It is natural."

When the girl came to me, I did not reproach her, but laid my mouth between her breasts.

"Comfort me," I said. "I have no refuge but in you."

I was cold and she warmed me.

"I know you do not love me," I said.

* * *

Solomon came to my chamber.

"No," I said, "I am not yet dead. You must wait a little longer. I am sorry to disappoint you.

He bowed politely. He treats me with an intolerable reverence.

I thought: why should Adonijah not be king after me, in place of Solomon? Why should he not wed Abishag when I am gone?

Solomon read my thoughts. He grew pale. He darted a look in which for the first time I read humanity: it was full of malice. Then the mask was resumed. He pretended that he did not know what I was thinking. He spoke solicitously. But, for a moment, he had wondered if he should take the pillow from behind my head, and smother me.

Are my nights a foretaste of death? I neither sleep nor am awake. Is that the condition of the dead, caught and condemned to dwell in a twilight world, in which the stirrings of the flesh are sad and weary memories, sad because no longer attainable, weary because of their persistence? In this half-world, I drift from the cold and lonely nights on the mountains of Judah, where the wolves howl, and the rough hair of my dogs presses against my limbs, to the sweet sweat that succeeded bed-wrestling with Jonathan. Michal reveals her nakedness and denies me possession. Bathsheba surrenders herself wholly to me that I may myself become her prisoner. And Absalom, whom I loved more than any other being, turns on me the sharp knives of his gaze and says, in the quiet voice of undeniable reality: "The son shall slay the father, for so it is written."

Abishag, in my withered arms, is all those I have loved, and none of them.

Laish presses himself against me, and murmurs: "If you had not been king, David, how happy we might have been," and the bloody head of Amasa, beautiful as all broken things, turns reproachful eyes on me, but finds no words to speak.

I heard a great cry from the city, a shout of acclamation, such as I had often known. But I did not know if it was in the city, or like my other voices.

So I lay there, helpless, like a little child who fears the terror of the night.

When Jonadab came to me, I did not dare to inquire as to the cry, lest there had been none.

"Why do you weep, my lord king?"

But I said nothing.

"Did the King hear a great clamour from the city?

"And is the King not anxious to know what it was?"

I thought: this is my creature. Yet there is mockery in his voice.

"Did my lord king not hear?"

"Samuel spoke to me," I said. "He made me the servant of the Lord and the instrument of His vengeance."

But perhaps I did not speak these words, for Jonadab continued as if I had said nothing.

"Adonijah," he said, "was preparing to name himself king. When Bathsheba the Queen heard of this, she had Solomon brought to the place before the Ark of the Covenant, and the priests at her command announced that you, being stricken in years, had appointed Solomon to reign in your stead, and to be king over all Israel and Judah."

"And Adonijah?"

"He has fled to a place of refuge, none knows whither."

So, I said or thought, Solomon has no need to kill me now.

I said: "I have no doubt you will serve Solomon as you have served me."

"Has the King any command for his servant?"

"Who am I to command?"

Surely, I thought, every man walks in a vain show. He piles up treasure and riches and does not know who shall gather them.

And now, Lord, Lord, what do I wait for?

I am a sojourner here, as all my fathers were, and I am ready for the long night and the darkness that covers all . . .

Epilogue ∫

These are the words of Ahimaaz, the son of Abiathar the priest:

The noble King David, the servant of the Lord, died having reigned forty years over Israel, seven in Hebron and thirty-three in Jerusalem.

And all the people mourned his death, and the chief mourner seemed to be Solomon the King.

Solomon reigned in his stead, and men believed that this was by David's wish and therefore accepted him. So none questioned his authority, even those who believed otherwise.

When Adonijah, the King's brother, whom David loved, sought the hand of his father's concubine, Abishag the Shunnamite, Solomon was jealous and ordered that his brother be put to death, and this was done straight away by the hand of Benaiah, the son of Jehoiada, a man of blood. And Solomon took Abishag, and raped her, and threw her on the streets as a common harlot.

Then Solomon turned on my father, Abiathar the priest, who had served David since he escaped the rage of Saul, and drove him into exile. He dared not kill him because he had borne the Ark of the Covenant into Jerusalem, but he exiled him because he was a friend of Adonijah the prince; yet declared that he did so to fulfil the word of the Lord concerning the house of Eli, which is the house of my father, in Shiloh.

But this was not true.

Then Solomon slew Shimei, who had cursed his father in the dark days of Absalom's rising against him, and declared that he had done so to avenge the insult to David; and that David had commanded him thus, for David had sworn to spare him in his own lifetime.

Solomon feared, I believe, being a timid man, that the tribe of Benjamin would hate him for Shimei's death, and therefore he cast the blame on to his father David.

Then Solomon sent Benaiah, the son of Jehoiada, against Joab, the general of the army. And Joab fled before him into the tabernacle of the Lord and clung to the horns of the altar, but Benaiah cut him down even there.

And again Solomon declared that in ordering this he was obeying the will of his father, even David, because Joab had murdered Abner and Amasa, and it was not fit that his hoary head go down to the grave in peace.

But I do not know if David had commanded thus, and whether Solomon spoke the truth about this matter. If he did so, it was not the whole truth, since, to David's mind, the greatest crime Joab committed was the murder of Absalom, his beloved son; and Solomon made no mention of that.

Therefore it seems to me that in this instance also Solomon lied.

Solomon also turned against his mother, even Bathsheba, and commanded her to retire from the palace and keep her own house, because she had urged him to favour Adonijah's suit for Abishag. She burst out in fury and swore he was the child of sin because she and David had wronged Uriah the Hittite, her first husband.

Then Solomon declared that the Lord had promised him great wealth and riches above that enjoyed by any man in Israel and had granted him wisdom excelling all others; and that, therefore, he would build a temple to the Lord, which was agreeable in the sight of the Lord, and which it had been forbidden to David to build, because he was a man of blood.

And so the temple of the Lord, like all Solomon's glory, was founded on a lie.

I, Ahimaaz, the son of Abiathar the priest, write these words in Egypt, whither I have fled from the vengeance of Solomon, though the agents of Benaiah the son of Jehoiada have pursued me even here, and would have slain me but for the protection of the Lord God of Israel, and other gods in whom I must needs trust while resident in this foreign land, that all may know through me that Solomon is a whited sepulchre, and that for his hypocrisy the Lord will bring his house in ruin to the ground notwithstanding the great and virtuous services of his father David, *whose testament I rescued from him, that all may know Solomon for what he is, and David for what he was.*

And I have set these words down in no malignity, but to do honour to the Lord of Hosts, whose name be blessed, by testifying to His truth which survives the words of men.

Exclusive CDs to enhance your reading pleasure

There is nothing better than a relaxing read and nothing quite like your favourite music to compliment your mood.

Each of the CD compilations are performed by the world's top artists. The choice is yours, all you need to do is send £1.98*per CD to cover postage and handling and indicate which CDs you would like. Please allow up to 28 days for delivery.

HOW TO GET YOUR CDS:
Simply complete the coupon below with the quantity of each CD you wish to purchase and send with your cheque to Hodder Headline CD offer, P.O. Box 2000, Romford, RM3 8GP.

Hodder Headline CD offer
Please send me:
Qty........HH01 Essential Opera @ £1.98 p&h each
Qty........HH02 Classical Masterpieces @ £1.98 p&h each
Qty........HH03 Rockin' n' Reading' Hits of the 60's @ £1.98 p&h each
Qty........HH04 Unmistakably Jazz @ £1.98 p&h each
Qty........HH05 Movie Sensations @ £1.98 p&h each
Qty........HH06 Gregorian Chants @ £1.98 p&h each
*Please note these prices apply to the UK addresses only. Please see below for other areas.

Enclose a cheque/postal order payable to FM LTD. Please write your name and address on the back of your cheque/postal order.

Name & Address...

....

....Postcode

POSTAGE AND HANDLING PAYMENT METHOD
UK & Ireland – Cheques or Postal Orders ONLY £1.98 per CD
Europe including Eire – Eurocheque in £Sterling ONLY or Visa/Mastercard Credit Cards £3.25 per CD
Rest of the World including USA and Canada – Eurocheque in £Sterling ONLY or Visa/Mastercard Credit Cards £4.25 per CD

Please debit £................ from my ☐ Visa ☐ Access

Card No

Expiry Date   Signature...

ENQUIRY HOTLINE: 01708 336888
If you do not wish to receive further mailings for products within the Hodder Headline Group or carefully selected companies please tick here. ☐ Offer subject to availability. Please allow up to 28 days for delivery.

Offer closes 31st December 1996   *you may photocopy this form*